THE SONSHIP SERIES

A Heart Alive

*Restoring the Truth about
our Spiritual Hearts*

By James Smith

©2025
A Heart Alive - by James Smith

Cover design - Carolyn Smith
Editor - Heather Hill
Book Design - Tom Carroll

ISBN: 978-0-6459271-2-2

All rights reserved. No part of this publication may be reproduced, stored in a retrieval system, or transmitted in any form or by any means – for example, electronic, photocopy, recording - without the prior written permission of the publisher. The only exception is brief quotation in printed reviews.

All scripture quotations, unless otherwise indicated, are taken from THE HOLY BIBLE, NEW INTERNATIONAL VERSION®, NIV®. Copyright © 1973, 1978, 1984, 2011 by Biblica, Inc. Copyright © 1982 by Thomas Nelson, Inc. Used by permission. All rights reserved.
Scripture quotations marked NKJV are taken from the New King James Version®. Copyright © 1982 by Thomas Nelson, Inc. Used by permission. All rights reserved.
Scripture quotations marked NLT are taken from the Holy Bible, New Living Translation. Copyright © 1996, 2004, 2015 by Tyndale House Foundation. Used by permission of Tyndale House Publishers, Carol Stream, Illinois 60188. All rights reserved.Some scripture quotations are taken from New King James Version®. Copyright © 1982 by Thomas Nelson, Inc. Used by permission. All rights reserved worldwide.

If you wish to contact me about anything in the book please contact:

theadventureoffaith@hotmail.com

Contents

Acknowledgements and Introduction … 7
Foreword … 9

1. Our Hearts … 11
2. The Life of God … 19
3. The Word and the Heart … 23
4. The Heart behind the Word … 31
5. The Hardening of the Heart … 38
6. Softening our Hearts and Repentance … 43
7. A Heartless Christianity … 49
8. The Orphan Heart … 53
9. What is heart forgiveness? … 65
10. Owning the Debt … 72
11. Getting back the Heart of Sonship … 76
12. Walking with God … 81
13. Fear or Love … 89
14. A Revival of the Heart … 92
15. The Heart and our Emotions … 96
16. Living from the Heart … 103
17. The Love of God … 109
18. The Heart and True Desire … 114

Footnote … 124
Final Thoughts … 126
Appendices … 128
Sources Referenced … 130

Acknowledgements and Introduction

I wrote my first book, "The Adventure of Faith", last year and I had no idea the impact that it would have. Whilst it's no best seller, people have written to me and told me that it touched their lives and encouraged them in their walk with God. This was food for my soul and has given me the motivation to write again on a subject close to me, *the heart*. The intention is that the book will be the first in a series of short books called the "Sonship Series". Let's see how that goes!

This book has been a slow burn for me, never really knowing when to end it. Just when I thought it might be finished more insight would come. This is the finished product within, I hope it encourages you and gives you a greater understanding of what God calls *our heart*.

I express deep gratitude to the teachers at FatherHeart Ministries, who put a plow through my theology in 2011, when *I thought I knew it all*. Whilst it was hard at the time, it has allowed me to see new things and in new ways, as I discovered who God my Father is. Thanks to Stephen Hill for affirming a writing gift in me and for helping guide me in how to get a book out. I express my deepest gratitude to Heather Hill (no relation to Stephen) for taking on this editing assignment amongst many competing commitments. My thanks to Tom Carroll for designing the book and to my wife Carolyn for the cover design.

And thank You to my friends and family for the encouragement to write again.

Foreword

We are living in the age of artificial intelligence, commonly known as AI. Never before has it been so easy to access information on all manner of subjects, including spiritual ones. It is tempting for me to think, "*Why write at all?*" All the information in the world is available with the click of a finger. "*Why spend hours writing about something that can be created in just moments?*" Then it struck me: AI can only present information; but, it can not express the *heart of God or the heart of a person*. AI is a soulless machine. God's word can never just be brought from a soleless entity, because it must be accompanied with His heart; And His heart can only ever be demonstrated through a human heart. After all, we are the ones *made in His image*. We, like God, are not soulless beings, but we have a heart, one which when surrendered to God can play the same tune that His heart plays. Our hearts are filters of both the good and bad, representing what is really going on in the deep places of our being. Machines can never be God's messengers alone; they *don't* and *can't* carry His heart. Only God's sons and daughters, His image bearers, carry His heart and can truly share His message.

So why a book on the spiritual heart?

Our hearts have often been dismissed as *just* emotional, deceptive and never to be trusted. But is that what God's word says? This book seeks to restore the truth about our heart. The *spiritual* heart is not the beating thing inside our chest; but, the very reality of *who* we are. Not just deceptive or evil - but, the carriers of God's life, where love and joy find their source. Our hearts are not something to be afraid of; but, when submitted to God they can carry: His very heart, His life and His love for humanity. The heart is the "wellspring of life", where our desire and motivation flow from.

May He reveal the truth of our hearts to us in a new way and may His heart become ours.

1. Our Hearts

A number of years ago a colleague of mine told me that "the heart is just wicked and deceptive". He could see no good thing about our hearts and he also had scriptural backing for this. Of course, he had taken this from **Jeremiah 17:9** (NKJ), which says, *"The heart is deceitful above all things, and desperately wicked: who can know it?"*. I later heard a popular international speaker say the same thing about the heart. The idea behind this is that only our minds' ability to interpret scripture and our will, are of any benefit in our walk with God. How far from the truth this is. This thinking can be partly attributed to modern education in which the brain is considered the centre of all thought and motivation; whereas, the heart is simply the 'ticking thing' inside our chest, keeping us alive.

Does scripture agree with this?

Jeremiah 17:9 has much truth in it, as does all scripture, there is no doubt that some very wicked ideas and thoughts have come from people's hearts. Even our own hearts are capable of wickedness. I have no doubt Hitler thought that the things in his heart for the nation of Germany were good and maybe even *godly,* as did his numerous supporters. So there is no doubt the heart can be deceptive and wicked. Thankfully for us there will be no horror movie made of the thoughts of our hearts - That would make for some uncomfortable viewing. However, the problem with thinking that our hearts are only evil and not to be trusted is nullified just two books later in the book of Ezekiel in which God says through the prophet: *"I will give you a new heart and put a new spirit in you; I will remove from you your heart of stone and give you a heart of flesh" (Ezekiel 36:26).* The old heart of stone has been removed from us and we are given soft hearts that can manifest the very life of God. Our hearts can be trusted when they are in submission to our Father and His love.

Secondly, even before Jeremiah makes this statement about our hearts being deceptive and wicked, the King of Israel, David, is chosen because of the goodness of his heart.

1 Samuel 16:7 (NKJ) says, *"For the Lord does not see as man sees; for man looks at the outward appearance,* **but the Lord looks at the heart."**

God said this in reference to His choice of person to be the next King of Israel. The King of Israel would be chosen by God *because* of his heart. Not only this, but God makes the audacious statement that David was *"a man after his own heart"* in **1 Samuel 13:14.** If God only saw our hearts as wicked and deceptive it seems unlikely He would say that He chose the King of Israel because he had a heart after His.

There is something about our heart and its connection to our Father in heaven. It appears our hearts need to be continually softened by the spirit and love of God. Discouragement and hurt inevitably come and as Christians our hearts become hardened through this: to God, to church and to other people. One of the most alarming end times scriptures can be found in **Matthew 24:12**, *"because of the increase of wickedness, the love of most will grow cold."* It is love that keeps our hearts softened to God and to others around us. You may know the scriptures back to front, yet, without love your heart will grow cold. We must stay connected to the Father in relationship, allowing His life to flow in us and through us. After all, knowledge when not accompanied with love just puffs us up, but it is His love that builds us up **(1 Corinthians 8:1)**. Allowing God's love to flow through our hearts is central to the battles that lie ahead of us. Knowledge is great; however we know from scripture that if we do not have love we will only sound like a clanging cymbal to a hurting and desperate world **(1 Corinthians 13:1)**.

May our hearts continue to be softened by the Holy Spirit on the long road ahead. As a church may we get an understanding of the heart as God sees it.

So what is our Heart?

The *spiritual* heart described in scripture is not the literal ticking, beating organ inside our chest. In fact, it's hard to put a physical location on the "heart" that is spoken of in scripture. The word heart or our *Spiritual* heart in the Old Testament comes from the Hebrew word **"Leb"** and refers to our "inner part or inner man". In the New Testament, it comes from the Greek word **"Cardia"**, meaning the "centre and seat of life". In other words, the heart is the very 'epicentre' of who we are, the source of life. It is our inner person and innermost thoughts. I like to describe it as: who we really are, our *truest* thoughts and feelings. James Jordan (**2012, p30**) says, "your heart is you".

Its other meaning is in reference to *taking* heart, and in this case it is the seat of courage or the source of courage.

We know that our heart and our Spirit are closely connected and at times their purpose and meaning appears to overlap (**Proverbs 17:22 NKJV and Exodus 35:21 NKJV**). However, it is clear that they are two separate things. God emphasised in **Ezekiel 36:26** that He would give us a new Heart and a new Spirit. Whilst both our Spirit and Heart appear to be part of our inner man and both affect our motives and desires, they are not the same thing.

It is surprising to me that so much of the teaching in the church in regard to our heart is about emotions or warnings about not being led by our hearts. I even recently read an article from a Western scholar saying that the only reason the Hebrew people attributed so much to the heart was because they did not understand that the brain was actually central to who we are and that we have now advanced this thinking **(Collins, 1995)**. On the contrary, I think the Hebrews had it right. The heart is the very *centre of us* - where life, motivation and desire truly comes from. Our mind works together with our heart and is extremely important too. But my emphasis is on the importance and centrality of our hearts as this has been lacking in the western church. It often seems the message in today's church is that, "You need to be afraid of your heart because it is a dangerous and deceitful thing". So what does God have to say about the heart? Apparently a lot, the heart is mentioned 824 times in the NKJ version of the Bible and is not all about emotions or how wicked our hearts are.

Below are just a few of the characteristics of the heart paraphrased from God's word:

Characteristics of the Heart:

- *It is where where our true life comes from (a "Wellspring' of life") **(Proverbs 4:23 NKJV)***

- *The heart is where desire comes from **(Psalm 20:4)***

- *From our heart comes our thoughts and attitudes - **(Hebrews 4:12)***

- *It is where God's commands can be hidden or written- (**Psalm 119:11, Proverbs 3:1. Proverbs 3:3**)*

- *We are called to guard our hearts and decide what we will allow into it. What we let in will affect the direction of our life. Note - we are called to GUARD our heart but not CLOSE it - (**Proverbs 4:23 NIV**)*

- *When we seek God with all of our heart, we will find him (**Jeremiah 29:13**)*

- *Our life reflects our heart (**Proverbs 27:19**)*

- *Salvation comes when the belief in our hearts and the words that come from our mouth are in alignment (**Romans 10:9**)*

- *When we believe in Jesus, out of the heart will flow rivers of living water (**John 7:38 NKJV**)*

- *What you say flows from your heart. What is stored up in your heart will come out in your words (**Luke 6:45**)*

- *When we trust the Lord with all our heart, he sets our path straight (**Proverbs 3:5**)*

- *The word of God judges the thoughts and intentions of our heart (**Proverbs 4:12**)*

- *The Lord looks at the heart as our true person and not at our outer appearance (**1 Samuel 16:7**)*

- *God works in our heart, creating a pure heart in us when we ask* (**Psalm 51:10**). *The pure in heart will see God* (**Matthew 5:8**)

- *The heart is a place that is deeply connected to our emotional state - A cheerful heart* (**Proverbs 17:22**). *A joyful heart* (**Ecclesiates 9:7**). *We can be brokenhearted and healing can take place here* (**Psalm 147:3**). *Anxiety can weigh it down but kind words can cheer it up* (**Proverbs 12:25**).

- *Our hearts can become hardened and dull, blinded to God's reality and unable to 'see' and 'understand'* (**John 12:40, Ephesians 4:18**)

- *When we lack hope or hope is delayed our hearts become sick* (**Proverbs 13:12**)

- *Understanding comes from our hearts (***Matthew 13:15, Mark 6:52***)*

- *Wisdom is found in the heart (***Proverbs 10:8***)*

- *Love is poured into our hearts from the Holy Spirit. (Romans 5:5)*

- *The heart is where we find the motivation and imagination for adultery (***Matthew 5:27-28***)*

- *Evil thoughts come from the heart - murder, adultery, sexual immorality, theft, lying and slander (***Matthew 15:19***)*

- *The heart can be evil, deceitful and beyond cure (**Jeremiah 17:9**)*

- *It is the place of motivation or intent for giving (**2 Corinthians 9:7**)*

- *God examines and tests our hearts (**1 Thessalonians 2:4 and Psalm 139:23**)*

- *Your heart contains your most important treasures or the things you love most (**Matthew 6:21**)*

- *It is where we find strength and take courage (**Psalm 31:24**)*

- *The origin for doubt is in the heart (**Mark 11:23**)*

- *We are called to love and serve God with all our heart (**1 Samuel 12:24, Mark 12:33**).*

Our hearts are rich store houses for the life and love of God to dwell and flow from. However, they can also become worn out, dull and unresponsive - unable to hear God and respond to Him. We would do well to listen to our hearts and know what they need.

2. *The Life of God*

Recently, I visited my friends who are running a church in New South Wales. They are amazing people who have literally laid down their lives to serve God. The church is only able to pay them a part time wage so they have to run several other businesses to live. Not only this but they homeschool their kids and run a climbing gym out of the church. So when I visited them, I was amazed with their commitment and love for the people they pastor. I could also sense this had come at great cost and that they were indeed *heavily burdened*.

At the end of the night I asked if I could pray for them and then I waited on God; hoping for some truly inspiring scripture or word that could bring them hope, or maybe even reveal to them some step they could take to help them. I was looking for a way to encourage them. As I waited on God for a word, I could only hear one thing, "Tell them that the most important part of this ministry is *their hearts."* I kept on waiting, hopeful for something more, but that was it. So I shared the word with them and prayed for them - hoping God might shine more light on the word. As I thought about that word later on, I began to see the truth and significance of it. We need programs, buildings and strategies; but, ultimately it is our hearts that carry the life of God **(Proverbs 4:23)**. Our hearts need to be cared for or they can become worn out, hurt and unable to share the life of God to others.

Our hearts are the containers for ministry. If they are not nourished, refreshed and revived then life can not flow through us. Our hearts are the filters for everything that flows from us, and like an oil filter in a car, when they become dirty it affects our whole life. We need to ask God to keep our hearts soft and responsive so that His life can flow from us. The Life of God is not found in our will or in our mind but it flows from our hearts. Often we judge God's word by asking, "is this biblically accurate?" But you would do well to ask the question; "Does this word contain God's life?" The heart of God is to bring life. After all He is *"the Way, the Truth and The Life"* **(John 14:6)**. The Amplified bible says that from the heart *"flow the Springs of Life"* **(Proverbs 4:23)**.

The Father has great investment in our hearts because it is there that the "Springs of Life" or *source* of life flows from.

Jesus said, *"a good man brings good things out of the good stored up in his heart, and an evil man brings evil things out of the evil stored up in his heart. For the* **mouth speaks what the heart is full of**" **(Luke 6:45)**.

He made it clear that it is the heart where life and death springs from. Good and evil both find their source in a person's heart. Again when questioned about food defiling someone, Jesus was quick to say that it is what is from within that defiles someone (their heart).

Jesus said, *"What comes out of a person is what defiles them. For it is from within, out of a person's heart, that evil thoughts come—sexual immorality, theft, murder, adultery, greed, malice, deceit, lewdness, envy, slander, arrogance and folly.* **All these evils come from inside and defile a person"** (Mark 7:20-23).

Are you beginning to see the importance of our hearts? It is where life and death and good and evil flow from. It is clear that what is stored in our hearts affects what comes out of us. I'm reluctant to use the expression, "we need to lead our hearts", although I know it is a very popular line in Christianity today. The idea of *leading* our hearts can be one in which we do everything by our will to ensure we never listen to our hearts. We can try to live almost separate from our true self because we develop an idea that "this is what I am supposed to *do* and *be*". That the heart is dangerous, deceptive and untrustworthy, so we need to live entirely from our willpower. I prefer to think of it as we need to *guard* or *consider* what we feed our hearts. We often think of things like lust, pornography and jealousy when we think of the sins of the heart and with good reason. But we often don't see how a worn out, tired, duty driven heart can also affect what comes out of us. If you have ever been through a really difficult season of life where you were exhausted by outward pressures you will know how this can affect the words and actions that come out of you. How you treat your heart will affect the "springs of life" that come forth from you.

When I was a young man I had in my mind how my life might look. Some of this has happened, but to be honest, much of how my life has turned out is entirely different. Jesus said in **John 10:10** that *"I have come that they may have life, and have it to the full."* We often think of a full life or an abundant life as coming from outside of us, i.e from the things we own and do. But the abundant life that Jesus spoke of is an 'inside job'. Overflowing life comes from within. We are told in **Proverbs 27:19** that *"one's life reflects the heart".* The life of God comes from our hearts and not from outside of us. When we are tired and empty the first thing we do is try and find things to fill us up. Movies, food, social interactions, name your filler of choice.... But the truth is we need the life and word of God to fill our hearts again. We would do well to remember that the life of God flows from the Father to us and then flows from our hearts to others.

3. The Word and the Heart

We need to acknowledge that our theology or understanding of God comes from two sources: **His word and the ground that it falls upon,** *our hearts* **(Matthew 13:1-23).** One of the things we need to understand with scripture is that we read it with our own filter; thus, we subconsciously filter the word through our own experiences and beliefs. We may think we are being very objective but we filter God's word according to our own heart; there is no pure filter for God's word. He works through us, regardless of the season of life we are in or how many 'kilometres we have on the clock'.

Yes scripture changes our hearts but our hearts also influence how we read and view the scriptures. We can have a very orphan hearted view of scripture and not even know it (more on that later).

Scripture does not come with a tone of voice; we create or interpret our *own* tone for it. For example, I have a very driven personality. I have what you might call an "A type" personality - I am very competitive and driven to get things done. This comes with advantages; however, I can also expect too much and be impatient with others. When I became a Christian rather than losing this driven nature, it simply became part of my new life. I was very driven to obey God; ensuring I was praying, reading the bible and sharing my faith enough to 'keep God happy'. I had what you might call an orphan heart (more on that later). Not only was I driven, I had the expectation that others would be equally driven. I thought if someone wasn't reading the bible enough or witnessing to others they weren't doing enough and I would become judgemental of them. Everything in my life was being interpreted through the lens of driveness and performance. When I read scripture what I heard was I had to *do more* and that the church wasn't *doing enough.* This only began to change years later when my heart received the revelation of sonship; I saw how I'd been living orphaned and outside of my Fathers love. I had inadvertently been working for the Fathers love and acceptance when I'd had it all along.

The Heart and the Word of God can never be separated as the heart is the soil for which the word falls upon. Jesus expresses this within a parable in **Matthew 13**, in which the same word fell upon four different soils: each a representation of the heart of man. On each soil there was a very different response to the word: One falls on very fertile soil and there is much fruit; another seed falls on somewhat fertile soil (rocky soil) but trouble and persecution affect its growth. Thirdly, seed falls on rocky soil but worries and the deceitfulness of wealth choke the word and make it unfruitful. Finally, some seed fell on hard soil, where there was no understanding of the word. In each of these scenarios the Word was the same but it was the condition of the heart (the soil) that affected the growth and fruit.

The Parable of the Sower - Matthew 13:1-23 NIV

> **13** *That same day Jesus went out of the house and sat by the lake.* **2** *Such large crowds gathered around him that he got into a boat and sat in it, while all the people stood on the shore.* **3** *Then he told them many things in parables, saying: "A farmer went out to sow his seed.* **4** *As he was scattering the seed, some fell along the path, and the birds came and ate it up.* **5** *Some fell on rocky places, where it did not have much soil. It sprang up quickly, because the soil was shallow.* **6** *But when the sun came up, the plants were scorched, and they withered because they had no root.* **7** *Other seed fell among thorns, which grew up and choked the plants.* **8** *Still other seed fell on good soil, where it produced a crop—a hundred, sixty or thirty times what was sown.* **9** *Whoever has ears, let them hear."*
>
> **0** *The disciples came to him and asked, "Why do you speak to the people in parables?"*
>
> **11** *He replied, "Because the knowledge of the secrets of the kingdom of heaven has been given to you, but*

not to them. *12 Whoever has will be given more, and they will have an abundance. Whoever does not have, even what they have will be taken from them. 13 This is why I speak to them in parables:*

"Though seeing, they do not see;
though hearing, they do not hear or understand.
14 In them is fulfilled the prophecy of Isaiah:
"'You will be ever hearing but never understanding;
you will be ever seeing but never perceiving.
15 For this people's heart has become calloused;
they hardly hear with their ears,
and they have closed their eyes.
Otherwise they might see with their eyes,
hear with their ears,
understand with their hearts
and turn, and I would heal them.'

16 But blessed are your eyes because they see, and your ears because they hear. 17 For truly I tell you, many prophets and righteous people longed to see what you see but did not see it, and to hear what you hear but did not hear it.

18 "Listen then to what the parable of the sower means: 19 When anyone hears the message about the kingdom and does not understand it, the evil one comes and snatches away what was sown in their heart. This is the seed sown along the path. 20 The seed falling on rocky ground refers to someone who

THE WORD AND THE HEART

hears the word and at once receives it with joy. ***21*** *But since they have no root, they last only a short time. When trouble or persecution comes because of the word, they quickly fall away.* ***22*** *The seed falling among the thorns refers to someone who hears the word, but the worries of this life and the deceitfulness of wealth choke the word, making it unfruitful.* ***23*** *But the seed falling on good soil refers to someone who hears the word and understands it. This is the one who produces a crop, yielding a hundred, sixty or thirty times what was sown."*

Jesus was adamant that the reason that people could not understand his message was because their hearts were calloused and hardened: "For **this people's heart has become calloused"** ***v15.*** He knew that understanding His Word was so much more than merely hearing words, it required a person's heart to be open to Him. Only a soft and open heart could receive an understanding of His Word as He intended it. Jesus could have just presented the facts and information about His Father and the Kingdom of God, instead He spoke in stories (parables) that the common man could understand. He tried to get past the intellect in which everything had to be w*orked out*, to instead speak to a person's heart where understanding comes through revelation.

There are two central things in our growth as Christians: *the Word and the condition of our heart.* That is why intellectual study alone will never result in growth as a Christian. Simply knowing the facts, the history and the context of God's word will alone not bring understanding. We need the Holy Spirit to shine His light upon us and open our hearts to hear what He is trying to say to us. That is why the Bible is such a fascinating book. You can read it thousands of times, yet the Holy Spirit can reveal something new to your heart - even when the stories are very familiar.

We also need to realise that having knowledge about God and having understanding are two different things. In **1 Kings 3:9,** Solomon asks for an *understanding* heart. Knowledge about something comes from study and our logical mind but true understanding comes from a deeper place, our hearts **(Matthew 13:15)**. We can get knowledge about something without really understanding it. I can remember when I was at school we had a group of exchange students from Hong Kong with us. They were awesome kids who worked really hard on their studies. I used to sit next to one young guy, Gordan, who would memorise huge chunks of text to help him pass subjects like History and Social Studies. English was his second language and at times it was clear he really didn't understand what he had written, but he could remember the text enough to help him pass. Similarly, you can have knowledge about God's word without having understanding. The bible is a spiritual book that can't just be worked out with logic and intellectual study. You might get past the first layer of meaning using your mind but there are many layers underneath that God wants to show us. Greater understanding of God's word comes when the Holy Spirit reveals something to our hearts. It comes through revelation, when we get that *"aha"* moment and all of a sudden we have a greater understanding of something. The bible is one book that is impossible to have *worked out* solely through academic study and our minds. It is a book of great mystery where God peels back layer after layer, showing us more about himself and the world around us as we walk with him.

The way we read and study scripture is often very different to how a Jewish person would read the "Torah". We often read the first layer of scripture and simply interpret the meaning based on our own knowledge and understanding. If we are wanting to go deeper we might study the original context of the word, look at the original meanings of the words in Hebrew or Greek or study the culture of the day to get a greater understanding. We in the western church might call this bible study. But this is not the way a Jewish person looked at the scriptures entirely. A Jewish rabbi might say, "*shivim panim laTorah*", which means; ***"there are 70 faces to the Torah"***. In other words the way they see scripture is like looking at a 70 faceted diamond. How you see it depends upon which way the light is reflecting on the diamond. Likewise, in scripture there are many levels of meaning and revelation to be discovered and enjoyed. There is much more than just one level of understanding and ways to see a scripture. The scripture was never meant to just have a historical or moral meaning, but it is *"living and active"* **(Hebrews 4:12).** There is often a hidden or mystical meaning that is peeled back by the Holy Spirit, but also a personal layer in which God chooses to speak straight to a person's heart and into their context.

You can not simply understand God's word through knowledge, but the Holy Spirit shines his light on it and brings life and meaning in many ways and during different seasons of our lives. Have you ever felt like God is highlighting a scripture to you in a particular season? This is the scripture being brought to life in you. Just like the light reflects off one face of the seventy faceted diamond at just the right time.

4. The Heart behind the Word

After about 7 years of being a Christian I had a moment of spiritual bankruptcy in my life. I had been doing everything I could to be a 'good Christian' and yet in my heart I was more judgemental and frustrated with people than ever. I knew lots about the word but my heart needed to change. Oneday, I had a revelation that God was my Father and I began to accept and experience more of his unconditional love for me. It was no longer about striving to be something or to have knowledge of something, but that I was accepted and loved by *someone*. We often forget that it is not our knowledge of the bible that demonstrates our relationship with God, but,*"by their fruit you will recognise them"* (**Matthew 7:20**). Knowing and reading the bible is important but this needs to be accompanied by a continuous experience of the Fathers love for us if we are to display the fruit of knowing him. Knowledge of the word must be accompanied by a changed heart, one that is living in the experience of the Fathers love for them.

Change is not just a matter of reading the Bible more. It is possible to read the Bible and know it very well and yet not know and demonstrate the heart that is behind the words. A person I worked with many years ago began to tell me about the church she attended. She told me how everything they do comes from scripture. For example, the Pastor would read large chunks of scripture to the congregation before he began any teaching and no teaching diverted from the passage or the context being studied. She also said that she personally read no other books except the bible to build her spiritual life. Her point was that her church was only influenced by God's word and not from other voices.

Now it sounds very spiritual to take our understanding of God only from scripture, we all probably desire this. The problem with this is our hearts will always affect what we hear and interpret from scripture. We are not robots in which information is simply inputted into us, our hearts are "deep waters" (**Proverbs 20:5**). The minute that scripture is read, we understand it according to our own heart. (For understanding comes from our heart - **Matthew 13:15**). Even if I made no personal interpretation or didn't add my own stories to God's Word but simply read a scripture passage to the audience, each person would hear something different.

For example, after I would preach at Youth with a Mission (YWAM) or church, people would often be keen to share what God had spoken to them about. Their *personal* revelation would often have very little to do with the main theme of my message or it would be centred on a tiny part of it - perhaps even a single scripture. This revelation had added to *their* understanding of what God was speaking to them about. I realised that God was speaking to each person's heart in a very *personal* way; their understanding came from the Word and their heart working together in beautiful harmony.

Conversely, God's Word can also be read and taught in a way that does not carry God's heart. Despite our best intentions, we can bring God's word without the motive or tone in which God intended. We may seek to bring the truth; but, when it does not carry God's heart it loses its true meaning. This is the deceptiveness of the orphan heart. For example, the Pharisees used God's word as a moral handbook to condemn others and promote their own self righteousness. They had forgotten that God's words needed to be filtered through His love and mercy for people.

When our hearts are not soft and open, the flow of God's life is blocked or at the very least restricted in its flow. God's Word and our hearts are always working together, you cannot separate them when it comes to our understanding of God. The perfect theology or understanding of God is not an intellectual thing and I don't believe getting our theology 'all right' is God's desire for us. The Father's desire is that we would be conformed into the image of Jesus (**Romans 8:29**); That our character and personality would become more like Him as His Word and Spirit transform us. Many of us think that one day we will have our theology ironed out and we can begin to share our revelation of God with others. But, our theology or our understanding of God will always be imperfect and intertwined with who we are. Our Father works in broken people and within their personalities. After all, God's power is made perfect not in our strength but in our weakness **(2 Corinthians 12:9)**. You will never have the perfect theology; but, you can let your light shine as you share your imperfect revelation that God has shared with your heart. It is why we do Christianity in community and are called to be one body in Christ, because one person never has *all* the revelation. It comes through all the body of Christ.

When we read the scriptures we cannot merely read its Words but we must consider the heart of the Father who inspired the entire message. His heart is the tone and the motivation behind the words that are written. His motive for everything was love; even though some might question this at times, especially in some Old Testament stories. We are told that *"God is Love"* in **1 John 4:16**. When God is described here, the author is not just using an adjective to say that God is: loving or faithful or compassionate; but He is using a noun to describe God. A noun is a concrete thing that you can touch and see. He is saying that the very heart of God, His very make up is love. So when you read scripture you have to interpret it through the filter of God's love. Even when Jesus showed anger or seemed to be blunt with

His words; He was motivated by His love for the Father and His love for the people He encountered.

One thing I learnt as a leader at a YWAM base in NZ is: that what we communicate is much more than the words that come from our mouths. People didn't always interpret what I said in the way I intended. After all, their own hearts were also at play and often I was inadvertently triggering their own hurts and disappointments. Conversely, sometimes what I said wasn't motivated by love. We can say and hear the right words but our motive, intent and understanding comes from our heart. If there is not an authenticity between our words and our motive, people will sense that. Likewise, the Word of God must be interpreted and motivated through the heart of God. When it is not, it may be the truth, but it will sound like a clanging cymbal to those around us. It may be the truth that sets us free but truth is best served with love **(Ephesians 4:15)**. How many of us have discovered in marriage that the truth without love can be damaging, bring division and separation. Truth and love must work together in harmony.

I can be a very direct person and I have spoken the truth as criticism and judgement many times. This has no value for the other person because when we criticise and judge it actually causes people's hearts to close up. Instead of opening someone's heart to hear God and potentially make a change, we actually cause them to shut down and become defensive. On the contrary, there have been times when I have had to bring a corrective word to someone, as have others to me. When this is done in prayer and with sensitivity to God's Spirit it can bring great breakthroughs. I remember bringing a word to a colleague I worked with in the past; I prayed a lot before I brought it and I presented it to him in *fear* and *trembling,* with no desire to bring division or hurt him. At the end of the year, this man came to me and thanked me. He said that word had saved him and brought him out of a lot of trouble. This is the truth and love working together.

We must also consider that *how* we say something is part of the message that people hear. Jesus tells us His Father not only told Him what to say but *how to say it* (**John 12:49-50 NLT**). Jesus knew that how He said something was part of the message that the Father was bringing. To connect with a person's heart, He knew that how He delivered the message was equally as important as the content of the message. Following His example, we must also consider not just the what of our message, but how we bring it. Often we can justify hurting someone by saying, "But it is the truth!" But until we have the love of God for people, the truth is just a swinging sword bringing division and hurt. Our hearts need to be filled with love as we bring forth the truth.

In summary, when we read the word we must understand that there is a heart behind it, the voice of a loving Father calling out to His children to be reconciled with

Him. God's word is received through the filter of our hearts, so there is never a 'pure word' from God. Once it reaches our heart it is filtered and processed in the soil of our hearts. Our hearts and God's word are working together in a beautiful synergy.

5. The Hardening of the Heart

Ephesians 4:18 *'They are darkened in their understanding and separated from the life of God because of the ignorance that is in them due to the* **hardening of their hearts**'

In the book of **Ephesians** it was the hardness of the peoples hearts that caused them to be "darkened in their understanding and separated from God's life". It is clear that our hearts can become hard to God and people. This causes God's life to no longer flow through us as He intends. When our hearts are hardened we can no longer see things as God sees them. We close ourselves off to what God wants to say to us and this impacts how we see others.

Pride and the hardening of our hearts go hand in hand. **James 4:6** says that, *"God opposes the proud but shows favour to the humble"*. This isn't a picture of God deliberately opposing and resisting people, that is never his heart. This is a picture of mankind's dependence on self and failure to listen to God, creating a block that prevents us from having a relationship with our Father in Heaven or at least listening to him. Pride and hardness of the heart go hand in hand.

Sometimes it is someone else's sin or even just the fact they are different from us that causes us to harden our heart towards them. We find it easy to identify the sin in others, but sometimes it's less easy to see our own sin and how it affects others. Maybe that's why God said to take the *"log from our own eye before we take the speck from our brother's eye"* (**Matthew 7:5**). Because the deceptiveness of our own heart means that when we are offended we can be 'one eyed', only seeing the sin of someone else and not our own sin and judgement. You don't have to be in a relationship long, especially a close one, before someone offends you or does something that upsets you. At this point, it is easy to harden our hearts and allow this to destroy the relationship. It is only the power of the cross and forgiveness that allows us to move forward, for our hearts to again soften to that person. Even harder, is when someone continues to sin against us time after time. We are not machines spitting out forgiveness tickets (more on this later), we do get hurt and offended. When this happens it is so easy to harden ourselves to someone. In a way the hardening of our heart is a way of protecting ourselves from a person and their sin. It is a natural response to sin and offence that is part of the fall. This is why Jesus encourages us to keep forgiving, He knows the deception of our hearts. He is also aware of our natural tendency to harden and close off to another person quickly when forgiveness is needed.

How often have you experienced judgement towards another because of their sin or the way they are? The closer that relationship is, the easier it is to see their 'true colours' and become their judge.

When I was single, I lived in a house with some good mates. One of my friends experienced depression which affected his whole life. He found it hard to go to work, sometimes spending large parts of the day in bed. I had prayed with him many times and nothing changed. I struggled with this. Why couldn't he just get free? Why did he continue to walk in depression? At times my concern went from caring for my friend to judgement of his life. My heart would harden itself, going from having a loving desire to see him helped, to a judgement of him. Eventually, my friend did get free and lived a good life; but, it was long after I had moved out. God works in His timing and His way.

God never hardens Himself to us - He is patient with us, wanting us to get free from the sin that entangles around us. God is always working with us, showing gentleness and compassion.

> **Jonah 4:2** *"I knew that you are a **gracious and compassionate God, slow to anger and abounding in love**, a God who relents from sending calamity."*

In the scripture we see the prophet Jonah discover again the mercy and compassion of God. Whilst Jonah had great judgement in his heart against the city of Nineveh and wanted God to punish the people; God was gracious and compassionate towards them, despite their sin. Yes, God will at some point judge Nineveh, as He will all people and nations; but, His desire is to *restore* all to Him. God's heart is full of compassion and love towards all people **(John 3:16).** Jonah's heart was not just hardened to others but to the whole nation of Nineveh. He wanted them to be punished, destroyed and there was a good reason for this. Likewise, our hearts can come into judgement of whole nations, people groups and organisations when offence comes.

During COVID, I was living in New Zealand (NZ). I have a large family of six children and the lockdowns were extremely difficult for us. It was probably one of the hardest seasons I have experienced. As a school teacher I was teaching my classes electronically from home, all the while trying to get my own three older children to do their learning, while two toddlers ran around and mum looked after the baby. As a family we like to get out into open spaces; but due to Covid apart from walking around the block, we couldn't do that. We couldn't even kick a ball at the local park. I also love going to the local cafe, not just for the coffee but for the chat. All these things were taken away for eight long weeks; my kids began to self-destruct and I ended up at the doctors with mental health issues for the first time in my life. I found this time extremely difficult and I got resentful and angry towards the Government for what we went through. Now, even if there were some good reasons to harden my heart towards the leaders of the NZ Government, this is not God's way. Later when we moved to Australia, I found myself having to forgive the leader of the NZ Government for that time in my life, releasing her from the things I felt she had inadvertently done against my family. Offence hardens our heart and blocks the life of God in us, even when the offence is justified. We can not justify unforgiveness and the hardening of our heart because, "we have good reasons for it". *The Kingdom of God works in a totally different way.*

We may even harden our hearts to someone who has a different theology or understanding of God to us. Their view is not necessarily wrong; but, because it's different from ours we harden our hearts to them. This creates walls between denominations and people of the same faith. It is possible to see something in a different way to someone and still have an open, soft heart towards them.

As you can see, our hearts can be deceptive and evil, continuously needing the love and life of God to soften them and help us forgive. We may be able to justify our hardened heart before man, but not according to God's word.

6. Softening our Hearts and Repentance

Many of us have been taught that to repent and turn to God: we simply need to *change our minds*. Of course, this is not completely wrong as one of the meanings of repentance comes from the word "metanoia", which can be interpreted to mean "changing one's mind". But, there is a lot more depth to the act of changing your mind than simply making a new decision about something, as we might understand it to mean. Even scholars agree that this interpretation misses the full meaning of repentance, as was intended in the original Greek. For example, we change our minds all the time: We decide to go to this shop instead of that shop; we decide to stay home instead of going out; or, we decide to go to this church instead of another. Of course this is not repentance but simply changing our mind; so, there must be *more* to repentance.

To understand the act of repentance more, you need to look at examples of repentance in the Bible. In one example found in **Joel 2:12-13,** the prophet urges the Israelites to *turn back to God with all of their hearts and to tear* *or to break their hearts* (paraphrased). They are not simply called to change their minds about something; but, to have a complete change of heart about their actions. Likewise, in the "Prodigal Son" parable in **Luke 15,** we see the son not just change his mind but his heart is softened to his Father as he has deep sorrow for what he has done. Repentance is as much a changing of your heart as it is your mind. It is the transformation of a person's heart towards God and others. A softening and opening of our heart to see now what is true.

The point I am trying to make here is that, often we are told that if we want to change the direction of our life we simply need to change our mind as in **Romans 12:2.** But, when you go deeper, you see that the heart of a person must be softened if change is to truly occur. Pharaoh continued to resist God because his heart was hardened to Him. This meant that even when his world and the whole of Egypt was crashing down around him, he still could not surrender to God. The Pharisees could not see Jesus as the Messiah and were blind to the things of God because their hearts were hardened and dull. This was not a case of simply changing their minds to see another way, but their hearts needed to be softened and enlightened so they could see and hear God.

A big part of Paul's mission was opening and enlightening the eyes of people's hearts to see and hear God (**Ephesians 1:17-18).** He prayed that *the eyes of people's hearts would* *be enlightened so they would know the hope they were called to* (paraphrased). Jesus also knew that to change a person, for them to experience genuine repentance, their hearts needed to change. He could have spoken straight to the minds of people producing a powerpoint presentation as to why the people needed a saviour and needed to change. Instead, He spoke in parables, knowing that a story could open and soften the heart and people could now have understanding, bringing genuine repentance.

It was the heart that was dimmed and closed in the Garden of Eden and it was the mission of both Jesus and Paul, and ultimately us, to illuminate and bring people's hearts to life again. For a person to truly change they must have their hearts softened and opened. We have taught people that to change all we need to do is give them new or better information - then they can renew their thoughts and move on. This is what modern education is built on: Give people the information about something and they will change their thinking. But you can't remove the heart from change. For years I taught as a secondary school Health and Physical Education teacher; I taught young people about the dangers of drugs, alcohol and unhealthy sexual activity. Then I went out and in my own time and acted out many of the behaviours I spoke against. This information had not changed me because my heart was still dull and resistant. I knew all the facts but that had not changed me from within. Many years later when I received an incredible filling of the Fathers love and accepted Jesus as my saviour, my heart changed as did many of these unhealthy behaviours and habits.

Often we can not understand why someone presented with the truth about Jesus will continue to resist Him and not commit their life to Him. How could such well presented arguments and evidence be resisted? But the truth is, until the heart is softened - as we see in the parable of the sower in **Matthew 13**- the word falls on hard ground and no understanding comes.

For years I shared with my Uncle about Jesus; as had my brother, my Dad, my best mate and countless others. There was simply hardness, resistance and counter arguments against God. One day at the Christian school I was teaching at in NZ a teacher came up and told me that she knew my Uncle from the UK very well, that she and her husband had known him for years. What a small world! Not much more was said about this until a couple of years later she told me that she and her husband were going back to the UK for a holiday and would be spending time with my Uncle. I was excited as she was a Science teacher and a Christian, so if anyone could convince my Uncle about God it would be her. After the holidays I was eager to talk to my colleague and ask how my Uncle had responded. I can always remember her opening comment, "Don't try and argue with your Uncle about God anymore, He already knows it all". My friend had shown him in a very scientific way how God had to be real and that there was much

SOFTENING OUR HEARTS AND REPENTANCE

evidence for Him. Yet he resisted every bit of evidence, his heart hardened to the truth of God. I knew then that only a softening of his heart would bring his defences down and allow him to let God in. All I could do was pray and have a relationship with my Uncle, as this was a matter of the heart, not intellectual debate.

A couple of years later I was offered a chance to go to an ANZAC conference in Turkey as a part of my work with Youth with a Mission (YWAM). The aim of the conference was to bring love and peace to the land, exactly 100 years after Australia and NZ had invaded its shores in World War 1. I gladly took the opportunity; but, I was also desperate to get the chance to go via the UK and visit my Uncle. I had a feeling this might be my last time. Amazingly, I did get that opportunity to visit my Uncle in London on the way over and spend a couple of days with him. I didn't get the chance to share about God; but as I left I asked if I could pray with him. By this point in his life he had some great difficulties and his heart had softened greatly. He said he was happy for me to pray for him. The wall of resistance had lowered and he had softened to God. I laid my hand on his chest asking God to help my Uncle, to bless him and to reveal himself to him. It was a simple prayer but even the fact that this hardened atheist was gladly receiving prayer from me was an amazing miracle. I then left and went on with my journey to Turkey. A few years later my Uncle passed away quite suddenly and I do not know where he was at in his faith journey with God; as we had not had another significant conversation after my time in the UK. I only know that his heart had softened to God and he was more open than he had ever been.

Intellectual arguments will never change someone unless accompanied with the love of the Father and the Holy Spirit softening the soil of the heart. It is easy to simply change your mind about something but to change a heart requires an act of God. In a way, to change our heart is an act of humility. One of the prayers I pray a lot now is to ask God to soften my heart, especially to another person. I can say I forgive a person and try to convince myself that they are a nice person, but until my heart softens to them it is difficult to show them mercy and the love of God.

7. A Heartless Christianity

Sometimes in the pursuit to *'be right'* we forget the heart behind the truth. We end up like modern day Pharisees, chasing the truth and wanting to be right, forgetting the heart of our Heavenly Father. We can become like the older brother in the parable of the Prodigal son: slaving away and never doing anything *wrong,* but unable to love a brother who was lost and is now found. We need to be careful that we don't end up living a *heartless Christianity.* The church is in need of a heart revival. We live in a day where information and ideas are everywhere but people need to feel a person's heart towards them; their kindness, love and care. Most importantly they need to know God's heart towards them.

God wanted the Israelites to be circumcised in the heart and not just in body. In **Jeremiah 4:4,** God says through the prophet, *"Circumcise yourselves to the Lord, circumcise your hearts, you people of Judah and inhabitants of Jerusalem".*

God wanted more than an outward sign of a relationship with Him. He wanted a heart change so they could feel His mercy, His love and even His pain for the world.

I believe metaphorically, God wants us to be circumcised in the heart too. To have our hearts broken and softened to what He feels and desires. Not just knowing God in an intellectual way with our minds, but seeing the world through His spiritual eyes and allowing Him to direct and lead our hearts.

Part of being circumcised in our hearts is living more wholeheartedly. Several years ago, when I was reading scripture the word *"wholeheartedly"* jumped out at me. There are at least twenty four instances in scripture where God uses this word wholeheartedly, with many more about seeking God with our whole heart. To live wholeheartedly really means to pursue or do something with everything within us, not impartially or disconnected from our true self. On this occasion I felt like God was wanting me to live in a more genuine way before Him and others, allowing my heart, who I am, to come out more. To live more authentically, not needing to push down everything that was going on inside me. The phrase "fake it to you make it" may be a popular catch phrase in our modern world but God sees the heart, the true intent and motive. There needs to be a genuineness between what is in our hearts and our words and actions.

I really enjoy listening to people preach. Most people like to stick to a script which is usually fairly safe, knowing that what they will say is acceptable to the group they are speaking to. But once the Holy Spirit comes on someone and they put the notes down you begin to hear what is truly in someone's heart, their passion you could say. Now you hear the real message come out, their real thoughts.

We live in a world where we are told what is *right* to say and what is *wrong* to say. Of course there is wisdom in keeping some thoughts where they belong, in captivity. But also hidden inside someone is the gold, that with permission will reveal their vulnerability and their heart. This is living wholeheartedly and it's where I believe God wants us to live. When I worked in a YWAM school where the participants were between 30 and 70 years old, we would give each person up to twenty five minutes to share their life testimony, usually people are given just a few minutes. This usually took two or three evenings in someone's lounge room but it was often the highlight of the school where many tears flowed and laughter was heard. For an older person to tell their story, twenty five minutes is nothing. It would often start slow but as they began to piece together the key moments of their life, a deep, holy moment would come across the room. People would begin to share their hardest moments and greatest trials, as well as their greatest victories. People would share what was really in their hearts and it gave others permission to be vulnerable and honest too. This is how we would begin our YWAM schools - *naked* (not literally) and *broken* before one another. In the environment this was done there was no judgement, just open hearts towards each other. This was for some a landmark moment where they could share wholeheartedly for the first time in a group. This has great power and strips us of our pride and strength and reveals the power of God at work in all of our lives.

Another example of *not* living wholeheartedly is when we try to direct everything we say by our will. Yes, this is necessary at times, but if we are not careful we end up living almost separately to what's really going on inside. Recently, I was speaking to a friend who started to really share her heart with me. She was sharing some disappointments with me about a situation she was in. Half way through speaking she almost stopped herself and said, "But, I guess I just need to be positive about it and get on with it". I stopped her and said, "It's actually okay to be honest sometimes, you know? You don't have to override everything that you really feel with positive will power." She looked at me relieved knowing that she didn't have to filter everything that she was really feeling.

When we live wholeheartedly we don't ignore what's going on inside. We might surrender it to God and we might show restraint and wisdom with it, but we acknowledge the reality of what is going on - the good, the bad and the ugly. Somehow God's making a beautiful tapestry out of it all.

8. The Orphan Heart

The word orphan is *only* mentioned by Jesus once. In John 14:18 Jesus says, **"I will not leave you as orphans; but I will come to you"**. When He said this He wasn't speaking to actual orphans, as we know for sure that at least some of the disciples had parents. He was instead referring to them and I believe us as well, as *Spiritual Orphans*.

Whilst the phrase 'orphan heart' is not mentioned specifically in the scriptures, the effects of the orphan heart echo from Adam and Eve, through human history and into our present lives. When sin came into the world, it seemed like a giant chasm opened up between us and God's perfect love. The freedom and acceptance that Adam and Eve once experienced in the garden seemed so much more difficult, if not impossible to access. The human heart became orphaned by the choice of sin, believing that we now had to do life on our own. Whilst Jesus came to reconcile us back to the Father, taking away sin and its consequences; the orphaned beliefs are so deeply ingrained in us that we can't simply say a prayer and it is gone. Yes, we are fully reconciled through Christ as God's children, but our hearts take a little more convincing.

Our core beliefs are anchored deeply in our hearts. They are not just fleeting thoughts that come and go; but they become the driving force behind our life. What we have believed, even subconsciously, becomes the motivation and filter for the way we see life - even read the scriptures. The orphan heart can drive everything we do, even though we may be *seeking the truth*.

The orphaned heart says:

"*I have to make it happen*"

"*I am on my own in this world*".

The orphan heart is the psyche behind much of modern day self help teaching: intrinsic and coming from our own resources. The problem is that nothing in this world can bring us genuine comfort or wholeness apart from the Fathers love. When Jesus left, He told His disciples He would not leave them as orphans. The word *orphan* in Bible times simply meant *Fatherless*, and one was considered an orphan even if their mother was still alive. This was because society was patriarchal and without a father the family was reliant upon either another man in the family or on the mercy of the community - it was a loss of position but also title when the father was gone. But the meaning of the word orphan in **John 14:18** also means **comfortless**. He would not leave them as *comfortless* but would give them the Holy Spirit; the Holy Spirit would be their *helper* and their *comforter* **(John 14:26)**, for the days ahead - as He is for us. Life throws plenty at us: both from the world and our own choices and we all need genuine comfort. Yes, there is comfort in this world that helps us: a hug, food, exercise, a great dinner or conversation with friends; but ultimately, we all need the Fathers comfort.

So where does that leave us? We can be a Christian but live in a very orphaned way. I know that because that is how I lived much of my Christian walk for many years. I tried very hard to be a 'great Christian' but would always be left thinking that I still needed to *do* and *be more*. I could never do enough and could never be the 'Spiritual giant' that I desired to be. My mission in life was to love God with all my energy. This sounds like a very biblical and holy desire, except it was one that I couldn't keep; it was like walking up a mountain that you can't quite get to the top of. You keep trying but there is always a bit further. I had forgotten that *"we love because He first loved us"* (**1 John 4:19**). Not just in a past sense; but, in the present sense. I can only love out of the love that I have and am receiving. You often hear stories of orphaned children coming into a family situation after a life filled with abandonment and pain. They have learned to truly live without a father and mother, without comfort. They may even become very hardened to life. As that child is loved and comforted by a father and mother again, gradually they can begin to express love to others again. If indeed they can accept it in their orphaned state. This is the same with us. We need the constant love of our Father in heaven - Not because we are extra needy or weak; but, because we are born into an orphaned world in which we all need a Father to comfort us.

When we have an orphan heart we will try with all of our strength to love God and others, but we have never learned to receive love. We try and do everything we can to be the 'best Christian' but because it is coming from an orphaned place, we are heading for disappointment and pain and ultimately *a crash*. Orphaned Christianity runs out of steam pretty quick. I know as I lived in it for my first seven years of Christianity, even today I am still being loved back to life. All the best communication and positive thinking techniques can not heal the orphaned heart. The orphan heart is only healed by allowing the Fathers love to flow into our hearts so that we can truly be His sons and daughters again. As we receive the revelation that we have His 'spirit of sonship', and live in this, we move out of a servant hearted Christianity - where we try our hardest to keep the master happy - and into one of intimacy as a son and daughter. We still serve but from the place of a *son*.

Jesus had no issue in obeying His father. He said in **John 4:34** that *"to do His Father's will was His food"*. It was the thing that nourished Him. He loved and longed to do it and He didn't see obeying the Father as something that was hard; or indeed that His Father was hard. His obedience came from a love response to His Father and not a fear of "keeping Dad off his back". As we come into sonship Christianity we too begin to move with the Father out of a place of love rather than military type obedience, which usually fails anyway. Often we talk about how hard it is to obey God. As we come into sonship I believe more and more we want to do what the Father wants. Not from a place of forced obedience, where we do something because we have to; but, from a place of love, knowing His heart for us and others is good.

The orphaned heart makes lots of bold statements about loving God and doing His work; but because it comes from a place of lack, an impoverished Spirit, it also comes with condemnation and self righteousness. When we get it right, which we will sometimes, we can't help but wonder why everyone else is not doing it like us. But when we get it wrong, it results in condemnation; eventually making more rules to try and get back to 'getting it right' again. The orphaned heart says all the right things, in fact sometimes it sounds so amazing. But it can't sustain its ambitions because it is not entrenched in the Fathers love. It often comes from a heart that simply needs to be loved.

When we close off our hearts and decide that only our intellect and our will is valuable in our walk with God, we prevent ourselves from being able to receive His love and comfort. In a way, we live in a comfortless Christianity, searching desperately to find false comforts: public rewards and recognition, addictions and and even using ministry to fill the love gap in our own lives.

When I finished as a leader with YWAM in 2018 it happened very quickly. I was planning to be the leader for another six months; yet, a day after a leadership meeting I stepped down. During my time at YWAM my heart had been changed by the love of the Father, many of my orphan ways had been revealed and were being loved back to life again. In YWAM I had taught people about a God that comforts us and loves us; not just in a theoretical way or simply at the cross, but in a constant and experiential way. I taught people that their identity was as a son to Father God and all our other forms of identity were trumped by this central revelation. As I stepped down all this was put to the test.

Had anything changed in me or was this just theory?

I went from being a leader with influence and purpose to having none of this, in just one day. This posed many questions for me: Am I first a ministry leader or am I a beloved son to my Heavenly Father? Whether I have influence or am publicly honoured and recognised, my standing in the Fathers eyes never changes. That's easy to say but when we find ourselves in testing situations it draws out what our real identity is.

I am a husband, a father, a friend, a teacher, a coach, a referee and many other things in this life; but, the only identity that remains and never changes, is my sonship to God. I am His and He is mine. This is my central identity which keeps all these other things in perspective. We all want influence and purpose in our lives and I do believe that God intends this for us, but it was never meant to give us our ultimate identity. Being a son or daughter to God the Father is our identity. Everything else is just a temporary role we get to perform here on earth.

The desire to be a spiritual leader is a noble one, but, when we have an orphan heart it can come from an unhealthy desire for *identity* and *to be seen*. After I went through bible college I had prophetic words over my life that I would lead a ministry and go to the nations. My heart was desperate for identity and to be validated, so these words could have easily become the driving force behind my life. The orphan heart finds it hard to be content and enjoy just being *us*. I know in my heart there was too much ambition and desire to be seen and have influence. When I discovered my primary identity was as a son to my Heavenly Father I began to see my relationship to him and my relationship to my family were the most important things in life. When my first ministry position didn't exactly turn out as I expected, I was in a good position to handle this because I now saw God as a loving Father, not a master only interested in the quality and extent of my work. My priority was to be a son to him and ministry was secondary to this. When I used to feel empty and lacking significance I would begin to think of all the things I should be *doing* or *doing more of*. Whether that was reading the bible more, sharing my faith or fasting and praying more. I related my need for intimacy and love with *doing*. If I could only live a life where I was always "doing the right thing", I would feel content in God. I now realise that emptiness was a cry of my heart for true intimacy with the Father. Not intimacy where I beat myself up for not reading enough or praying enough but where I go to the Father and find rest, love and peace in Him. Anything He needs me to *do* comes from a place of rest and not condemnation and restless demands.

Another symptom of an orphan heart is living behind our 'fig leaves'. These fig leaves represent the things that we use to comfort ourselves or protect ourselves so others never get to really see us. We live from the person we think we should be or maybe the person others think we should be. We try very hard to keep up appearances and our Christianity is simply hard work. In other words we put on an act to hide our real person from others. We don't let our heart come out because the real us is: messy, unfinished and imperfect. What if others really knew me? What if they knew I was insecure? Afraid? Unable? Angry? Still struggling with addiction or unforgiveness?

Our fig leaves mean that our heart and our actions are never in sync with one another and we use all our willpower to keep up our act.

What if the only way to heal the orphan heart was to get our identity as His sons and daughters back, to live in a place where being loved is our central purpose of living?

The Solution?

> **Matthew 7:9-11** *"Which of you, if your son asks for bread, will give him a stone? Or if he asks for a fish, will give him a snake?* **If you, then, though you are evil, know how to give good gifts to your children, how much more will your Father in heaven give good gifts to those who ask him!"**

I have a great Dad in so many respects. He has prayed for me my whole life, supported me in all my endeavours and was extremely generous to me and still is. But when I was in my teenage years I saw things very differently. Dad was a gentle man who wasn't into the outdoors and playing sports and he wasn't like many of the other Fathers I knew who would build a shed and drink beer. And to make matters more conflicting: I was a difficult kid.

So, I had a lot of judgement about my Dad and my heart closed off to him emotionally for many years. When I lived overseas for three years from age 24 to 27, I expected that being away from my Dad would help me heal. But, I could still feel the pain of separation, the judgement and unforgiveness in my own heart, it was overwhelming.

The heart of what I will share next comes predominantly out of the revelation that James Jordan, the founder of FatherHeart ministries in NZ shares in his teaching. Jordan says that *the only way we can get the heart of a son back is by restoring our 'heart of sonship' that we lost somewhere along the way* (**My paraphrase - Jordan, 2012, p91**). This of course goes back to our first experience of being a son or a daughter to our parents. For some this was not a good experience, and it is true for all of us that none of us had a perfect experience in being fathered and mothered. Many of us have had abusive, absent or passive fathers who simply did not share the heart of our heavenly Father. Some were blessed with a dad who shared many aspects of the Heavenly Father's heart and in an incomplete way they were able to get a glimpse of how the Father sees them. Some simply didn't have a father. Whatever your experience, our response to our fathers and mothers is something we live with today. Therefore, for some of us we shut down or reject being fathered or mothered because of all the pain this caused. Shutting down is a part of being a fallen human and since the fall we have all closed down our heart in some way to avoid pain. Inadvertently, when we do this we also shut off our ability to be fathered and mothered by God. We shut down our hearts and declare: "why would I want another father when the last one hurt me so bad?" Even with good fathers, sometimes what we have experienced does not reflect our Heavenly Fathers heart towards us. (Note - If it sounds like there is somewhat a focus on our earthly fathers more than mothers, it is because in my experience most often the pain and separation comes from Fathers.)

So how do we get the heart of sonship back?

We don't stop having an orphan heart by trying hard not to have it. We get the heart of sonship back when we begin to walk as sons and daughters again, with God as our Father. Often this means we have to go back to where we lost our heart of sonship. Usually this was with our parents, as I described before, often with good reason. We have pulled back and said: "I will never allow someone to hurt me like that again"! I found that to get back the heart of being a son to God the Father again, I had to go back to the relationship I lost with my earthly Father. I wrote a long letter to my Dad not long after I became a Christian and we were able to sit and talk about what I needed but couldn't get from him. I realised he couldn't give me some of the things I needed because he hadn't received them either. I was able to release my dad from any debt I felt he owed me and I was able to ask forgiveness for the way I treated him as his son. My heart began to open up to him again after that day. But it also allowed me to be fathered by God in a new way. It probably took another year or so; but, eventually I got to a point where I had no pain or resentment in my heart towards my dad anymore. I could accept him totally for who he was, appreciating all the great things he had given me as a Father. Since this time my dad has become one of my greatest friends and I no longer have judgement in my heart towards him.

I can remember one day when we were visiting my parents in Sydney I asked my Dad whether he would give me a Fathers blessing. He laid his hand on my head and declared his blessing over me. It was another moment which changed the trajectory of my life. My relationship had been restored with Dad. I could also be fathered by God and begin to live from a place of sonship and not from a place of orphan hearted Christianity, in which I was insecure and afraid of a harsh and unpredictable Heavenly Father.

For many people they can not restore their relationship with their earthly parents; the reality is that may not be a safe option; or maybe they have even passed away. Perhaps they do not know them anymore; or maybe a discussion about the past would see them pushed further away. However, we can still release our parents from the debt we feel they owe us, with the help of the Holy Spirit, despite reconciliation not being a possibility.

9. What is heart forgiveness?

Matthew 18:21-35

Then Peter came to Jesus and asked, "Lord, how many times shall I forgive my brother or sister who sins against me? Up to seven times?"

22 Jesus answered, "I tell you, not seven times, but seventy-seven times.

23 "Therefore, the kingdom of heaven is like a king who wanted to settle accounts with his servants. 24 As he began the settlement, a man who owed him ten thousand bags of gold was brought to him. 25 Since he was not able to pay, the master ordered that he and his wife and his children and all that he had be sold to repay the debt.

26 "At this the servant fell on his knees before him. 'Be patient with me,' he begged, 'and I will pay back everything.' 27 The servant's master took pity on him, cancelled the debt and let him go.

28 "But when that servant went out, he found one of his fellow servants who owed him a hundred silver coins. He grabbed him and began to choke him. 'Pay back what you owe me!' he demanded.

29 "His fellow servant fell to his knees and begged him, 'Be patient with me, and I will pay it back.'

30 "But he refused. Instead, he went off and had the man thrown into prison until he could pay the debt. 31 When the other servants saw what had happened, they were outraged and went and told their master everything that had happened.

32 "Then the master called the servant in. 'You wicked servant,' he said, 'I cancelled all that debt of yours because you begged me to. 33 Shouldn't you have had mercy on your fellow servant just as I had on you?' **34 In anger his master handed him over to the jailers to be tortured, until he should pay back all he owed. 35 "This is how my heavenly Father will treat each of you unless you forgive your brother or sister <u>from your heart.</u>"**

One of the most recognised scriptures dealing with forgiveness is found in **Matthew 18**. There is much in the passage in regards to forgiveness and the unlimited mercy of God and His call for us to share this same mercy to others.

WHAT IS HEART FORGIVENESS?

Less is made of the ending of the scripture which says: that if we do not show mercy and grant forgiveness to our brothers and sisters, we would be like the tortured, unmerciful servant **v34**. In other words if we couldn't forgive our brothers and sisters, we too would live in a kind of internal torture. As a Christian, even just as a human, we all have experienced this turmoil. As we hold onto the debts of others, plotting revenge in our minds, we realise that we become the victim of this internal torture as we lose our peace. Meanwhile, the perpetrator is none the wiser or simply unrepentant.

Another aspect of this is that we are told that we need to *"forgive our brother or sister from our heart"* v35. We are not just called to forgive, but to *forgive from the heart*. So what does it mean to forgive from the heart?

As I have already mentioned, the heart is our inner person: our deepest thoughts and desires that make up the real us. When God calls us to forgive from the heart, He calls us to truly forgive from our whole being and not just say a few words because we have to. We are often taught that to forgive is simply a choice we make. Whilst this is undoubtedly the first step in forgiveness, like repentance, there is more than just making a choice in our minds to forgive or even saying the words "I forgive you".

I think most Christians know that the appropriate response in this life is to forgive someone. Most of us would identify that forgiveness is the heart of the Father with Jesus being the greatest demonstration of this by going to the cross and forgiving our sin. However, often our ability to forgive only goes skin deep. For example, if we continue to walk around with hatred and thoughts of revenge towards a person who has offended us, you can guarantee that we have not truly forgiven from our hearts, yet. Heart forgiveness is a journey. It starts with a choice and ends when we no longer have any thought of revenge or anger in our hearts towards a person. This can take time and no doubt comes with pain. I can remember when we lived in NZ, a friend of mine hurt me greatly. I knew that my response was to forgive him so I made the choice to do so. The problem was everytime this person's name was spoken, the thoughts of anger would rise up in me. I wanted to say, "If only you really knew that person, you would not want anything to do with them". I was in inner turmoil or torture everytime I thought of that person. Finally, one day I was driving in the same suburb as where my friend lived and anger rose up as I thought of him.

God spoke to me clearly that morning, "You have not forgiven this person, James"

"Yes I have Lord. I made a choice months ago to forgive them", I replied in my mind.

"You have not forgiven this man from your heart", was the thought that came.

WHAT IS HEART FORGIVENESS?

I felt immediate conviction in response to what the Lord had spoken. Yes, I had made a choice to forgive and I wanted to forgive; but, I was still in inner turmoil and torturing myself over this man's actions. I had not forgiven him from my heart. I began to pray about how I could release this man fully from my heart. Two things came to mind which have helped me many times since: I needed to pray for blessing over my friend, asking God to help me soften my heart towards him. Secondly, I needed to continue to ask God to help me release him from the debt that I felt he owed me.

After this, whenever the anger rose up I began to pray for him, blessing him, even though this was against what my feelings were. I also asked the Lord to soften my heart towards my friend and help me to fully release the debt that I felt he owed me. Eventually I visited my friend, taking with me a gift and card. On the card I had written that I was hurt by what he had done and had struggled to forgive him but that I wanted to do this now. I then spoke a blessing over him.

He never owned his actions nor apologised to me; yet, from that moment on I was able to begin to fully release him from his actions against me. I continued to pray for blessing over him and release him whenever anger or thoughts of revenge came up in my heart against him. Eventually, I came to a point where I no longer held anything against this person. I was free and the debt had been released. I had forgiven him from my heart. I was never able to fully restore the friendship but I could now walk in freedom and know that there was no debt that he owed me. This is forgiveness from the heart.

When we forgive from the heart we are totally free from pain and they are free from our judgement. I don't say this flippantly as I know the pain that offence can inflict. Nor can I experience your pain or anyone else's; but, I know that God would not have asked us to forgive if He couldn't help us to do it. Heart forgiveness comes from deep within, hence why it's so painful.

The story in Matthew 18 teaches us another thing. The debt we release another from pales in significance compared to the debt God has released us from. When we can see that, it helps keep what has been stolen from us in perspective.

The man in the parable above was forgiven of millions of dollars of debt; yet, could not release his servant from just a few thousand dollars of debt (*the amounts in* **Matthew 18** *have been changed to the modern day equivalent*). The debt that someone owes us may only be equivalent to a few thousand dollars, but the truth is, it does cost us. But, it is still tiny compared to what God the Father has released us from. This perspective can help us let go of what is owed to us.

WHAT IS HEART FORGIVENESS?

Forgiveness releases us from inner turmoil and torture. But it is more than just a flippant choice. It goes to the level of our heart and we need God's help to do it. We need to continue to ask God to soften our hearts and help us release the debt we believe that someone owes us. Also, by praying His blessing over the person it can help us move from inner turmoil and tortured feelings to peace. That is heart forgiveness.

10. Owning the Debt

Another important part of heart forgiveness is to actually own and identify the debt that is owed to us. In the story above, the master and the servant both took account of what was owed to them. When you know what has been stolen from you, you are aware of the debt that you need to release. My friend Barry tells a story to highlight why we should identify the debt owed to us first:

Barry is a farmer on a beautiful farm in the South Island of New Zealand. Occasionally, he would have workers come out to the farm to help out. One day one of his ex-workers returned to visit him, saying that he was sorry but when he had worked for him he had taken some things from his shed and had not told him. In other words he had stolen from him. Barry being a Christian man accepted his apology and forgave him. Over the next little while Barry would go to the shed to get a tool and was frustrated that the tool was no longer there. It was then he remembered what the worker had told him about taking 'some things'. He then began to question, "What else did he take from me?" Barry had forgiven the man for a debt, but he did not really know what it was. He now wishes that he could go back and actually ask him what he had taken, so he could see what the debt that was owed to him was and on that basis release him.

Interestingly, Jesus never tells us that forgiveness will involve justice. Sometimes we go through things and we are paid back for what has happened or the perpetrator receives a consequence. Sometimes, we also may receive an apology. But Jesus never says that forgiveness would involve earthly justice. In fact, the hardest debts are the ones that are not or can never be paid back. To let a debt go when you feel like another person has gotten off the hook is difficult. We want justice; but, forgiveness trumps justice. At the end of the day, complete justice was achieved by Jesus Christ on the cross. He forgave my sin, your sin and your perpetrators' sin. Yes, our hearts will still cry out for justice on earth. We don't want to see the thief go unpunished or the person who hurt us never come back and apologise. But at the end of the day, many times we won't get justice here on earth and Jesus still calls us to release the debt. This is where forgiveness from the heart becomes real. I am not going to get paid back for what has been taken from me, but I am still going to release this person from their debt. This is perhaps the greatest sacrifice and challenge we will ever face on this earth.

Forgiveness is more than just a choice, but it is releasing someone from our whole being until their name or thoughts of them no longer disturbs our peace. This is the process of forgiving our brother from our heart.

Forgiving our parents can be like this. Our parents can never pay us back for the mistakes they have often inadvertently made. For the most part our parents did their best but had their own limitations, hurts and pain to deal with. Because of wounds from our parents many people carry unforgiveness around in their hearts and shut off their hearts to being *fathered* and *mothered*. More often it is their father that people have forgiveness issues with, but not always. When we ran YWAM schools we had a ministry time where students were invited to write a letter to their parents, which usually was never sent to them (**See appendix 1 for an example**). The letter was for the writer's benefit and not for the parents. The letter would be about acknowledging the blessings that their parents gave them, but also recognising the things that they could or did not give them and the pain this had caused. They needed to feel these things, they were often painful and deep and in many cases had led to issues in their own adulthood. It wasn't 'playing the victim' or blaming parents for their life. But it was acknowledging the debt that was owed to them but could never be paid back. It was holding it again and acknowledging their parents' lack, so they could let it go. When people went back into these painful moments it was there they could make a choice to let go of these debts. For some it involved deep and painful emotions, but afterwards, there was often freedom and a new way of seeing things.

During this process people would get into small groups and read the letters out, considering the debt that was owed to them. They could now make a choice to let their parents go and forgive them from their heart. Those around them would pray and speak words of encouragement over them. Some people experienced instant release from unforgiveness and for others it began the journey of letting go. Some wanted to write letters of thanks to their parents afterwards. For some it began a new relationship with their parents, but for others this wasn't possible and yet forgiveness could still occur in their own heart.

But something happened that people didn't expect; When they forgave their parents, more often than not their hearts began to open up to being a son or daughter to God again. They got back the *'heart of sonship'* and they could now relate to God, not just as the saviour, but as "Abba Father" or 'Daddy God'. This revolutionised their relationship with God. They saw a side of God that they never knew existed. A new bookcase full of books was opened up to them.

11. Getting back the Heart of Sonship

Galatians 4:4-7

"But when the set time had fully come, God sent his Son, born of a woman, born under the law, to redeem those under the law, that we might receive adoption to sonship. Because you are his sons, God sent the Spirit of his Son into our hearts, the Spirit who calls out, "Abba, Father." So you are no longer a slave, but God's child; and since you are his child, God has made you also an heir."

Whilst writing this book, a friend requested I write out the steps of how we go from having an 'orphan heart' to a 'heart of sonship'. (Note - the word 'Sonship' incorporates both male and female, even though the word is masculine).

It would be easy to say: here are the ten steps; but, then I would essentially be saying that this is an intellectual exercise, which it is not. It is a circumcision, a cutting, deep in our hearts that has to happen. It begins when we realise that many of our life's activities have been influenced by our orphaness. That our orphaness is deeply ingrained in us, echoing back to the garden where perfect intimacy and relationship was broken. We may even have borne much fruit in our life, but we know something is missing. We've had a revelation of Jesus as our saviour and the Holy Spirit as helper; but, if we are honest we don't know God as "Abba"; As 'Pappa'; or 'Daddy' as the word really means. There is a longing within us to know God as an intimate Father who truly loves us in a way that supersedes anything we can *do for Him*. That Jesus was the *way* to the Father and not the destination. By living in Jesus and by Him living in us, He would reveal God as "Abba". Abba loved us way before we had any capacity to love Him. The source of love is not in us, but in *Abba, Father*. That *"we love because he first loved us"* (**1 John 4:19**).

Sonship began with the realisation that I was desperate for acceptance and that I was restless in my heart, looking for validation and to be known as a 'great Christian'. I needed to come out of my restless striving and into rest. Sonship was the great undoing of me. It was also the discovery and acceptance of my weakness. It was seeing myself as a child of God who desperately needed a Father. That I was loved, despite my weakness and failure.

I had to come to realise that my relationship to my parents affected the way I saw God as a Father. I have already spoken about heart forgiveness and restoring the heart of sonship. I needed my heart restored to them as a son, so I could be a son to my Heavenly Father too. This also helped me see authority in a new way and began a journey of no longer seeing leadership as a *threat* and with *suspicion*. That authority was not always the opposition, trying to hold me back from the plans of God. That I could honour authority again, albeit, in an imperfect way.

I began to see God's word in a completely new way. Knowing the Father meant I wasn't living condemned all the time for not being good enough; or doing enough. For a long time, God's word had seemed like a book of commands and directives. But now it is no longer demanding or simply directive but it is *affirming* and *comforting*.

I was being called out to live from the "Tree of Life" (see footnote), in a relationship with the Father that had been completely restored because of what Jesus had done on the cross for me. It began a journey of living more authentically, accepting weakness as part of my walk with Him **(2 Corinthians 12:9)**. Knowing that God enjoyed living in me and working through me despite my weaknesses, flaws and failures. That He was firstly a God of love - yes holy, just and righteous, but these were all governed by His love and not the other way around, as I had always believed. God is "LOVE" and not just loving (**1 John 4:8)**. God is Holy because He is *perfect love*; and love can not and does not sin. The Father was Holy, set apart from any other living thing because He always lived from love and had no alter ego like we do. He has no sin nature and is always motivated by love. In **Romans 13:10** it says, "*love is the fulfilment* *of the law"*. In other words when we are motivated by God's love in every action and thought, we will not sin. Many don't want to overstate love in their churches and their preaching because they have come to believe that love is permissive and too liberal. That we need to keep reminding people that God is Holy in case God's love leads them into sin and doing *whatever they want*. This is because we have made love into a human construct, that we are the source of love. God's love always delivers us from sin and does not lead us into it. We can only love from the love we receive from God and not by willpower and good will. If we have God's love in our hearts we will be Holy. It is not one against the other.

As my heart was awoken into sonship I began to learn to live in the experience and truth of the Fathers love for me. I had to get used to the idea of being continuously loved and living in that experience, as that is what heaven is like. I had always seen God as so driven and harsh, like a slave driver. Some of these things had to be undone in me.

It meant that *performance* and *perfection* had to go in my life. I have always been a person to "give my best" and "give everything a go", and I always will be. But when I thought that I had to perform or do things perfectly for God, I resisted the grace of God in my life. I lived in constant condemnation, always wondering: "how could I do more and be better". I could never just accept where I was on the journey with the Father.

The Father began to teach me to walk as a son to Him. Not worrying about ministry or position, but enjoying my position and identity as a son to Him. As I did this there were ministry opportunities and fruit, but it was coming from a different place - it was the Father who was initiating it.

The *lost* became people who could be my friends and be loved by me, and not just people who needed my evangelism or 'notches on my belt', if you like. I could live not thinking I had to convert every person I crossed paths with.

I began to see things through new eyes and this is a continuing process and not an arrival. The FatherHeart teachers used to say that teaching sonship was like a 4 year old teaching a 3 year old. A child doesn't pretend to have all the answers but is happy to share the ones they have. Sonship is becoming childlike and learning to live like this in our hearts again. It is the beginning and not the arrival. It is the continuous unravelling of our orphan hearts, our flesh if you like.

This is the best I can do to describe the steps of moving into a heart of sonship and coming out of our orphaness.

12. Walking with God

Studying the scriptures and walking with God are not the same thing. King David was a man who walked with God. He knew and loved the scriptures, but he did so because they spoke of the God he loved and was getting to know.

Psalm 25:4-5

Show me your ways, Lord,

teach me your paths.

Guide me in your truth and teach me,

for you are God my Saviour.

David's love for God's word was a pursuit of knowing God more. This is very different to studying the scriptures so we can make sure we 'get it all right', or to use them solely as a moral handbook. Sometimes our greatest spiritual ambition can be to make sure that we have our theology all locked down and without any error. That is not walking in freedom with God. I remember a young man telling me that after he left bible college he could no longer sit through a sermon without judging every word that came from the speaker's mouth. He could no longer receive and relax in the word because he had to judge and critique every word with his now growing knowledge of scripture. How sad is that? Yes, we judge the word but from a totally different tree, the "Tree of Life". We ask ourselves, "Is this word in line with God's heart?" This moves us beyond the fickle assessment of every word with the question: "is this right?" or "is this wrong?"

Someone can bring a word that's full of the Bible; but, it may not reflect the heart of God. This was the issue with the Pharisees and Sadducees. Likewise, you can make a statement that isn't printed in black and white in scripture; yet, it reflects the heart of God. Just because we say something is in the Bible does not mean that it carries God's heart. Let me explain this with a human example: I might say something in a certain way or within the context of a bigger conversation- I might even say it with a smile on my face or in a joking way- which is very common in Australian culture. Now if someone else hears that without seeing the smile on my face or knowing that it was said as a joke, they could hear it very differently then what I intended. (My wife is always onto me about my Aussie sarcasm.) Or maybe I say something with a great deal of concern and care for someone; But again, if you didn't hear the tone and see the care in my face it could be taken in a totally different way. Likewise with God's word, the heart behind the word is so important. For example, when I first started preaching, I would sometimes get a word and would think, "person x really needs to hear this today". In other words, I felt it was my job to judge and correct a person with the word I had been given. It was uncanny that whenever I did this, the person who I had decided it was for would be away that day. The word may have been good; but, my heart was wrong. It was not my job to judge people of sin. We bring a word anointed by the Holy Spirit and He decides how He uses this word in other people. The heart behind the word contributes tremendously to our message.

It is interesting to think about how Jesus used the word whilst He was on earth. He did not use His words to accuse or condemn people. As I read the Gospels, I see Jesus' indignant anger and strongest words reserved for the hard, unbelieving hearts of the Pharisees. They could see the beautiful fruit of healing, salvation and restoration that Jesus brought and yet refused to acknowledge that this was from God. They were stuck living from the "Tree of the Knowledge of Good and Evil", assessing everything as right or wrong according to their small minded understanding of God. This Spirit is still alive in Christiandem today. Unable to see the beautiful fruit of God because it does not fit into our exact theological box, even using scripture to undermine the works of God. It was Jesus who said that, *"by your fruits you will know them"* **(Mark 7:20)**. Some have defined this fruit as having our understanding of scripture perfectly worked out and packaged. That is not the heart of the Father or the fruits he speaks of........ *"But* *the fruit of the Spirit is* **love, joy, peace, forbearance, kindness, goodness, faithfulness, gentleness and self-control.** <u>Against such things there is no law".</u> **(Galatians 5:22-23)**.

When Jesus revealed someone's sin, He could be direct but also speak with great love and gentleness. This allowed the listener to truly hear and receive it. An example of this was with the woman at the well (**John 4:1-29**):

Although Jesus was very direct about her sin, He brought it without condemnation, to let her know that He could see her fully and yet He was not deterred from loving her. When she could feel and see the love that Jesus had for her, she was able to get free from her sin.

Accusation never brings freedom. When Jesus was stern and forceful about sin He was coming up against the religious spirit in the Pharisees. The people whose greatest sin was thinking that what they were doing represented the Father's heart and yet was far from it. But with the crowds, He shared parables and let the word itself convict someone of their sin. He spoke the word and let people work out for themselves if this was for them. Jesus wanted people to identify that they needed a saviour and let the Holy Spirit and their own hearts convict them of this. Jesus had every right to use His words to accuse and condemn people for their sin, after all, "He knew no sin". He could have been the first to cast a stone at the lady who was caught in adultery, but He chose to not condemn her.

Often we use the Bereans in **Acts 17**, to justify wrongful judgement and unbelief when receiving God's word from a speaker or pastor. But the Bereans were doing something very different when they *"examined the scriptures every day"* vii. In Acts 17 it says that the Bereans *"received the word with all readiness"* from Paul and Silas and afterwards went away to examine the scriptures. They judged by their spirit that the word Paul and Silas brought was indeed from God. But, they then went away and searched the Old Testament scriptures to see if this *new revelation* was in step with the truth they already had. They did not have a New Testament Bible as we do, so the words that Paul and Silas were speaking were not being checked or cross examined as we might understand. They were examining the Old Testament scriptures to find a witness to what they had already received and welcomed in their hearts from Paul and Silas through the Holy Spirit. This is different to someone shutting down everything a speaker or pastor is saying because they preach from a different version of the bible from them or are offended by a small part of their message. They were not using the scriptures to check that every little bit of their theology was *right* or in perfect context, finding fault and closing down their hearts to what God was wanting to say. Instead we find in v12 that, **"As a result (of this faith), many of them believed"**. Their hearts were open and receptive to God's truth. They were hearing with faith and the scriptures confirmed that the revelation they received was in step with the Spirit of God.

Our quest to be *right* about God can seem like it is a very Holy thing; but so often it comes from a hard, unbelieving heart that seeks to find fault in others' words. Often people will bring a word that has God's heart in it and we can sense that. The theology may actually be incomplete; but, God still anoints the word. We live from the "Tree of Life", learning more about God as we walk with Him and enjoy His word. We don't live from the "Tree of the Knowledge of Good and Evil", having to have it all right before we can share with others about Him. A word may be full of life and hope, but someone may shut down from it because of their own unbelief. This was not the heart of the Bereans as some may understand it to be.

The scriptures are a reflection of God's heart and character. The Bible is meant to lead us into a closer and more certain relationship with God. It was never meant to be a study of the intellect, in which we are determined to get our view of God 'all right'. As we walk in relationship with Him, we do get to know Him better, but through revelation. We undoubtedly change our view of who He is; but this comes from knowing Him and by Him revealing new things to our hearts. God shares himself through revelation (Him revealing things to us by His Spirit), and not by us trying hard to work it all out. **1 Corinthians 2:9-10** says, *"these are the things God has **revealed to us by His Spirit**".*

As Christians sometimes we can be afraid to truly express who we believe God to be, because we might get something wrong: This is a relationship of fear. A relationship that I refuse to partake in any more. This finds its source in the "Tree of the Knowledge of Good and Evil" and not from the "Tree of life". I know my understanding of God is incomplete; I know others have revelation about parts of His character that I do not know; and, that is absolutely fine. Often people come under great criticism for getting something *wrong* from scripture. Like the Pharisees with Jesus, we wait for someone to make a mistake and condemn them by their words. God does bring correction to our lives and He does use others to show us this. (**Proverbs 27:17** *'As iron sharpens iron, so one person sharpens another'*). But, He does not condemn us when we make a mistake or don't have it all worked out. He works with us and enjoys a relationship with us. He is not looking to expose us because we have got a verse out of context or have not fully understood the scriptures. He looks at our hearts. Do we have humility and are we teachable?

There is error in all our theology. We can walk freely with God knowing that we don't have the full picture but that He is faithful to show us more. The error that we should be most concerned about is the error that comes from a hardened, unloving heart. For example, when someone uses scripture in a way that reveals what is really in their hearts, whether that be greed, or desire for power, or judgement, or pride.

In our modern society we often consider maturity as a Christian to be measured by how much we *know*. What if maturity as a Christian was actually becoming more 'childlike'? I don't mean childish as in becoming more self centred or short tempered, but childlike; as expressed in **Matthew 18:3**.

Jesus said, *"Truly I tell you, unless you change and become like little children, you will never enter the kingdom of heaven."*

Jesus was referring to an attitude of the heart: Humble, teachable and believing. A heart that can express love, joy and the other fruits of the Spirit. A heart that knows it isn't all knowing *about* God, but is at rest in that, not even making that their ultimate goal.

As we walk in community, we should not walk in fear of getting it wrong. But, have our eyes set on God and knowing Him more, letting Him steer us along the right track. When our hearts are soft and open to Him, He can give us revelation to see Him more clearly than we did before.

13. *Fear or Love*

Our response to what we hear and how we act is directly linked to what is in our heart. Is it fear or is it love driving us? Often a mixture of both. The way we interpret God's word or even interpret a situation is directly linked to what's in our heart. Two people can hear the same news and one can interpret it as a threat and the other as something very different. When love comes into our hearts, our response to God's word and all of life's challenges completely changes.

Think of Stephen who was stoned in **Acts 7**. We might consider him as a courageous man for standing his ground against evil men and speaking the truth. No doubt that this was an act of immense courage, but in **Acts 7:55** we see the reason for his courage…."But Stephen, **full of the Holy Spirit,** *looked up to heaven and saw the glory of God, and Jesus standing at the right hand of God.".*

Stephen was full of the Spirit, in other words he was full of the love of God. Because "God is Love" (**1 John 4:8**), when we are full of His Spirit, we are full of the Father's love. Stephen could show such courage because his heart was filled with love.

Not long after I had left bible college in Tauranga, New Zealand, I was given a word by one of my Pastors that, "I was to do the work of an evangelist and to do this I was not to have even a pin prick of fear in me". The word was meant as an encouragement and I took it as that, however how my heart received it didn't always play out well in the future. Whenever I experienced fear in my heart, which I did regularly, I would think "I can't have fear in me" and would begin to condemn myself, leading to more fear and anxiety. It is the love of God that *"casts out (removes) all fear"* (**1 John 4:18**) and not our own bravado or courage. When fear came I wasn't to condemn myself, as God understood my weak flesh, but I was to go to God and *"cast all my cares on him because he cares for me"* (**1 Peter 5:7**). I needed His love and comfort at this time and no motivational speech or self help mantra was going to take away my fears. When I spoke from a place of faith expressing itself in love, I was able to move without fear. But my carnal nature would always experience fear and anxiety.

Another situation where what was in my heart influenced the way I saw something was with my neighbours. I have always been a sensitive sleeper who wakes up easily when there is noise. I had some bad experiences in NZ with neighbours who had kept me up at night. Because of this I began to think of my neighbours as a *threat* rather than a blessing. Inadvertently, this affected any future neighbours we had and triggered anxiety when I heard any kind of noise. It was not a relaxing way to live. It got to the point where I decided I needed to get some prayer for my anxiety around neighbours. It was when I was getting prayer that I received the word, "you are seeing your neighbours as a threat and God wants to change the way you see them". In other words God wanted to change my heart perception from one of fear to one of love. Not long after this I felt like buying my neighbour's some dinner from the local pizza place. At that point we were not very close with them and had only had a few conversations and I still predominantly considered them a *threat*. I delivered the food and they were really grateful for this. It felt like a prophetic act for me. One in which I was demonstrating that my neighbours are a blessing and are not a threat. After that time my heart began to change towards my neighbours. I began to enjoy conversations with them and my wife (Carolyn) and I looked for ways we could be a blessing to them. They also began to do the same to us. My heart began to see my neighbours from the place of love and not fear. This doesn't mean that there will never be problems with neighbours or conversations might be needed, but that can come from the place of love.

The way we hear and see things will always be influenced by our hearts. Fear can cause us to see and hear things differently than when our hearts are full of love.

14. A Revival of the Heart

Acts 2:42-47 "*They devoted themselves to the apostles' teaching and to fellowship, to the breaking of bread and to prayer. Everyone was filled with awe at the many wonders and signs performed by the apostles. All the believers were together and had everything in common. They sold property and possessions to give to anyone who had need. Every day they continued to meet together in the temple courts. They broke bread in their homes and ate together with glad and sincere hearts, praising God and enjoying the favour of all the people. And the Lord added to their number daily those who were being saved*"

The Christian church began in revival in **Acts 2**. Great boldness and love came upon the first disciples as they shared the gospel message far and wide, with people being added to the church daily. There have been other significant revivals since the experience of the first church and I love reading about the sheer numbers of people turning back to Christ, the miracles and the joy experienced. But we also need to consider how the hearts of people are revived by the Spirit of God in times like these. The love of God fills people's hearts and the fear of man begins to disappear. Of course this happens not just in times of church revival, but when the church is in revival there are a great number of people experiencing revival in their hearts together.

The church is in great need of a heart revival. When people's hearts are revived there will be a natural outpouring of love, joy, peace, patience, kindness, gentleness, faithfulness, goodness and self control. You can never work your way through determination into these fruits. They flow from the Father's heart into ours. We can steward them and be intentional with them, but the fruit comes from our relationship with God. When people's hearts are changed there will be salvation, miracles and works of unconditional love. No preacher will need to convince people to do these things because *love* will compel people. People will want to know God's word and they will want to share their faith and pray for the sick etc.

The New Testament scriptures were written by people living in revival. Living in a time when there was a great outpouring of the Spirit and love, where the church was growing and miracles were commonplace. To fully understand and live the scriptures out, our hearts need to be in revival too. For most Western Christians who have been following the Lord for a long time, knowledge is not a problem. Most Christians know enough scripture. But this is different to when God really reveals himself through scripture and the scripture becomes "living and active", working through us and moving beyond just an intellectual truth. Many of us pray for revival and for good reason. I too want to see a revival in the Christian church. But the greatest revival will be the one that occurs in us, in our hearts.

When I left Faith Bible College in NZ my heart was alive. I was filled with the desire to share God's word, pray for the sick and do the works of God. I was compelled by the love in my heart and God's Spirit to do these things. I quickly realised, however, that many Christians in the church were not in this place. They were not doing these things and nor did they seem to desire too. I can assure you that this was not because people did not know enough scripture. I don't write that as a criticism because since that time I have been in dry places and have at times lost the desire to do God's work. I write it to say that knowing God's word alone will not compel people into works of love. They may feel condemned and think, "I should be doing these things" or "why aren't I doing these things", but that does not lead to good fruit. Only the Spirit of God refreshing our hearts and compelling us through love will cause people to truly live in the word of God. Otherwise it just remains an intellectual exercise where we study and know the bible but the fruit is not there. That is why our hearts need a revival that comes from the Holy Spirit. When God compels someone to move, the fruit will be so much more beautiful than when someone attempts to do God's works from their own willpower or a motive of fear.

15. The Heart and our Emotions

We need to remember that our hearts and emotions are not the same thing or the same word in scripture. Our emotions are totally separate from our hearts and our hearts are much more than the centre of our emotions. However, there is no doubt there is a connection between our hearts and our emotions. For example scripture describes our hearts as being: cheerful, joyful and even anxious. But there is also a connection between our heart and our words **(Luke 6:45)**, and our heart and our thoughts and motives **(Hebrews 4:12)**.

When someone says that our hearts are only about emotions, or that our emotions are our hearts, that would not be Biblical. However, if our hearts are the very centre of who we are, then there is little wonder that the condition of our hearts is connected to our emotions. Our emotions are like an alarm system to show us what is going on in our inner man **(Proverbs 13:12)**. Emotions shouldn't lead us in a reactionary type of way, but they are valuable and are a gift from God to help us. We are emotional beings, sometimes our emotions clearly are an over reaction and cannot be relied upon. However, if we constantly ignore emotions we are quite possibly ignoring the warning signals that our heart is sick and we need to take action.

Oftentimes we are taught only to relate to God in our logical minds, that He is somehow against any kind of expression of emotions. Our emotions are a good thing. They help us express the fruits of the Spirit: love, joy, peace, patience, kindness, goodness, faithfulness, gentleness and self-control. Our emotions also help us express unrighteous anger, frustration and pain. When they are shut down or told they are of no use, we close off this central part of our physical and spiritual life.

David had no problems truly expressing his emotions to the Father: **Psalm 55:4-6** is just one example of David expressing negative emotions to God.

> *My heart is in anguish within me;*
>
> *the terrors of death have fallen on me.*
>
> *Fear and trembling have beset me;*
>
> *horror has overwhelmed me.*
>
> *I said, "Oh, that I had the wings of a dove!*
>
> *I would fly away and be at rest.*

Or in **Psalm 22:1** he says, "*My God, my God, why have you forsaken me?*"

He also expressed positive emotions towards God. In **Psalm 119:47** he says, *"how I delight in your commands. How I love them!"*

God is concerned with the whole human experience; David had no problems expressing anger, frustration, sadness; as well as delight, joy and love to the Father. It appears the Father had no problems with this either as it has become part of the scriptures, written in the Psalms. David wasn't led by emotions, he was led by God. His emotions weren't there to lead him but they were there to help him identify and deal with the different seasons that make up a human life.

God wants us to have an authentic connection with Him and this includes being able to express real life emotions; without this, our relationship can become robotic and unauthentic. An authentic relationship with God means we can be real with God and express how we feel.

If we want to have a heart connection to the Father, then emotions will at times overflow as He touches our heart. This may mean that someone is touched by God and tears begin to flow in His presence or even uncontainable laughter happens. One of my friends became very embarrassed because when he would go up and get prayed for in our church in NZ, he would sometimes get overwhelmed by emotion and would laugh hysterically for many minutes. It was a release of emotion and joy for him which could only come from a touch of the Fathers love. He was concerned

THE HEART AND OUR EMOTIONS

because his parents had neither experienced this, nor would connect it to God, as some people reading this may not. This young man was being touched at an emotional level by his Father in heaven. Not through words or study, but Spirit to Spirit - heart to heart. It is important to understand that God does not just have a logical mind, but He also has emotions and created them in us. The problem with emotional connection may not be that, "it isn't in the Bible", but that we haven't yet learnt to experience life in our hearts and live from that place with God. When this is the case, any interaction outside of our logical mind can not be understood and we won't connect it to God.

A couple of years ago I was in a really desperate place and needed a touch from God. At that time an evangelistic campaign called "The Tent of Promise" was going on in a town close to where we live. When I heard about it I felt I had to get there and that maybe God could touch me. At the very least I could get some prayer. When I arrived with my son I shared with a young guy that I was going through some trials and needed prayer. He prayed for me and my son and I also received counsel from a wise, older man. They encouraged me to come back later that night as they would be having a church service of sorts. So, later that night I joined a small group of people in worship and heard an evangelistic message. It was nothing out of the ordinary but at the conclusion we were encouraged to join together for prayer. We held hands in a circle and prayed in a group of about fifteen people. As we did something broke in me and I began to laugh hysterically. The man next to me, a local pastor, saw that God was doing something in me and turned to me, laying his hand on my chest. Again more laughter for the next several minutes. It was a beautiful refreshment that I was experiencing and so much joy was released in me. More importantly, I walked away from that meeting in a totally new place in my heart. God had brought me out of a very difficult place. It drew me closer to God and gave me renewed desire to seek his word, but it wasn't a permanent touch from heaven, just a temporary touch of God bringing me out of something that I couldn't get myself out of. Sometimes we are afraid of emotional experiences with God but a true touch of God brings refreshment and deliverance.

Many people love to worship God through music because they get an encounter with God that touches the heart and bypasses the logical mind. Comparatively, others who would never connect their emotions to God can watch a movie and have an outpouring of emotion. That is because stories are powerful and they touch our hearts and connect with our emotions - getting behind our walls. Isn't that why Jesus spoke in parables? He knew understanding could not come from the mind alone, but that a person's heart needed to be touched and enlightened.

I am the first to admit, I have not been amazing at teaching my own kids the Bible stories. When they were young they all sat and read bible stories with me, but having six kids has meant that, at times, this has faded by the wayside; particularly as they got older. No doubt knowing the stories of the Bible are important for kids to learn; but, I believe equally as important is to express love to our kids in tangible ways so they learn how Father God wants to express love to them.

The love deficit we all received as children from our parents (to some degree), can be restored to us- no doubt. But I believe when we show our kids how loved they are through: words, touch, time, gifts and acts of service; we allow their hearts to be able to receive the love of Father God much more easily. How painful it is for a child who never was shown love in a tangible way or only through correction? They may even come to believe that God's way of expressing love is only through correction or by being directive, because that is how their parents modelled love. They may have never been shown affection and so they can not make the connection between God the Father and affectionate and affirming love.

In the book by John Arnott titled *"The Father's Blessing"*, (1996), the author describes his experience of watching the love of God move from simply a theoretical belief for many, to an actual experience of receiving the Fathers love in a tangible way. This resulted in what many call "The Toronto Blessing". In his book he affirms what I am saying here when he says, "*if parents would only emotionally touch and hold and affirm their children, they would grow up much better prepared to respond to the love of God. Our hearts need to know how wonderful God is and how much he really cares for us. This revelation needs to reach deep into our inner beings".* **(Arnott, 1996, P25).**

We often think of the inheritance of God as passing down the stories and knowledge about God to our children. No doubt this is an important part of inheritance and it helps children understand who God is. But, when the stories and knowledge are not accompanied with an experience of the kind of love that the Father has for them, this can be confusing. Yes, they know the story and the commands of God; but, they can not relate to the love of a wonderful Father as this has not been demonstrated to them. When our kids see and hear the love of God through our voices, our facial expressions and our actions they get a taste of who their Heavenly Father is.

God was not afraid to express emotions and He created them in us. We need to be able to relate to God in our hearts and through emotion as well as through scripture and using our minds.

16. Living from the Heart

Often you hear the expression, "to go with what's in your heart" or "live from the heart". What do we mean by that? And is this a sinful statement? When we use this expression we are usually meaning that we are going to do something that is in response to what we truly believe, or that is in line with who we genuinely are. The way in which most Christians use this expression is when they are excited to be doing something they love, or know they need to follow. In other words, to do something that is really important to them and that comes from a true expression of themselves. Of course when this is sinful or in disobedience to God, we have a problem. Our hearts are always under the Lordship of the Holy Spirit; if someone lets their heart lead them over scripture and the guidance of the Holy Spirit, it is death to them. We might say, "I'm going to go with my heart and…: cheat on my tax, or divorce my wife, or quit something God wants me to stay in"; this is the deception of the orphan heart that Jeremiah speaks of in **Jeremiah 17:9**.

Scripture is clear that we are led by the Spirit **(Galatians 8:14)** and that the word of God is the sword or weapon of our Spirit (**Ephesians 6:17**). However, when most people use the phrase "I am going with my heart", they are not usually using it in a sinful way. They are saying, "I am going to respond with what I feel is right in my inner man"; this should always be submitted to God and guided by the Holy Spirit. Many Christians use this expression in an innocent and God honouring way. Often they will use it when they feel like God is unlocking something in them and showing something of who they truly are. They are not using the expression to go against God's word; but, in a way of expressing the desires of the heart that God is giving to them. So the statement "to go with what's in your heart" is a neutral one. A person could use this statement to pursue evil just as someone might say this to pursue something that God has put on their heart to do.

Likewise, we often hear the expression that someone has a 'good heart'. What do we really mean by that? Sometimes people will express something in a less than perfect way; but, because we know them or have had previous experiences with them, we understand that the motive or intent of that person is essentially *good*. It is a statement that says, "I know who you truly are and I know that your intent towards me is good."

Have you felt misunderstood by someone for something you did or said when you felt your motive was good? I am certain most married people would nod their heads to this. I can remember after I got married that I would do things for my wife that I would have loved to have received from her. The only problem was that some of these weren't well received by her as they didn't speak *love* to her. When I needed touch and conversation, she needed peace and quiet. My motive and my heart towards her may have been 'good', but I needed to learn what would speak love to her heart.

For our hearts to remain soft and our intentions good we need to keep allowing the Holy Spirit to soften us. I believe it is one of the enemy's tactics: to harden our hearts towards people and even life. When this happens we may know the truth of God; but, it is difficult to have His motive and His intentions towards others.

If you want to truly know God and share Him with others, you have to connect with Him on a heart to heart level. Only then can you know His heart. Knowing His word is one thing; but, when you know His heart towards his word, then you can see as He sees. You can have compassion and empathy for others as you catch God's heart for the world.

It is when we live from our hearts and in connection to God's heart that we feel most alive. I have always loved the bush, exploring it by walking, running or cycling and searching for wildlife (more on that later). But when I became a Christian, it was like this interest took on a new life. Going out in the bush and on walks became incredible times when I would connect with God the Father.

Sometimes I would have intense times of prayer and intercession while walking in the bush. I can remember praying for my marriage on one occasion in such an intense way as I walked. I would profess the truth of our marriage through scripture, declaring it to the Heavenly realm as I walked. It felt like an opening of heaven and that God was right there with me encouraging me as I walked. Other times, it would be a time of incredible download where I felt like the Father was sharing something with me about my future and it came like a movie track to me.

When I was at Bible College I would spend one day a week fasting till 4pm and I would spend my lunch time praying for my friends and family. Later in the afternoon I would break the fast by riding through beautiful scenery to a nearby coffee shop. As I rode back and with nothing left to say it was often then that God would speak to me through my thoughts in such a clear way. It was like now my mind was still and I had stopped talking, He was free to speak to me. I really enjoyed those downloads riding back to the college as I came back full of God's thoughts and imagination.

I would also often practise preaching a message as I walked in the bush, often a message that I hadn't begun planning for yet, so it was coming straight from my heart. Finally, sometimes it felt like God just wanted to hang out with me in a place I loved and He loved too. Not long after I became a Christian I took a trip to NZ. When I got to a place called Queenstown, I discovered that there was a place I could go mountain biking. I had done very little 'proper' mountain biking in Australia and had simply used my mountain bike to get around the streets. So, I somewhat nervously hired a bike and headed to this world class mountain biking forest. For the next five or six hours I went down all kinds of tracks, including the hardest, 'black trails'; at times feeling like I might not make it out alive, falling over the handlebars several times. But, what I remember most about that trip is sitting in the middle of this beautiful forest, eating my lunch, reading the scriptures, and talking to God. It felt like God the Father was right there next to me at that moment. I was a new Christian and this kind of interaction was so precious to me. I would not have associated this connection and intimacy with God before. But this was His day out as well and He was going to use it to build a friendship with me. What kind of God wants to have a friendship with us? I was discovering that this God was indeed wanting to be my closest friend.

When I am dry or desperate or I feel far from God, I still to this day head out into the bush or wild places to meet with Him again. I never come back disappointed as He meets with me and pours life, love and encouragement into me again. My adventure times with God in the bush or at the beach have become such treasures to me. It is there that I learnt to have a heart to heart connection with God. Not just a transactional one in which I can repeat bible verses, although I enjoy that too and believe it builds my faith. But, a heart to heart friendship connection where the God of the Universe, my Father in heaven, chooses to walk side by side with me, sharing a conversation as we go.

God the Father wants a heart to heart connection with us that can only happen when we relate to God in our hearts and learn to connect emotionally with Him. Our hearts are a place not only to connect with Him emotionally but also to receive love from Him. A loved heart can not only receive love, but can share love too.

17. The Love of God

Have you ever been to a conference or listened to a speaker, even had an amazing worship time and walked out of it feeling full of God's love? We often relate to being in God's presence with the mental stimulation it provides. We might say, "what a great word that was" or "God really spoke to me through that". But what if it wasn't just about mental stimulation but also about God depositing love from His heart to ours? In **Romans 5:5** it says that *"God's love has been **poured out into our hearts** through the Holy Spirit, who has been given to us."* What if God's love was being "poured into our hearts" when we are in His presence? What if that was why we felt different when we came out of that conference or worship session or after we had spent time with Him?

Our western culture often considers our relationship with God as simply a mental one, where we read and learn about God and the events of the Bible. But, I believe Christianity is also a transaction that takes place, where God deposits himself into our Spirits and into our hearts. As this happens we take on more of His personality and His character and are transformed into His image **(2 Corinthians 3:18)**.

I remember my Pastor in Tauranga, Andy Turner, asking me how I thought my preaching went after I shared a word to the church. I might have said something like, "It seemed to go okay."

He would then reply, "There were lots of great conversations going on afterwards, people wanted to hang around and fellowship, so it must have been good" (my paraphrase).

At first I didn't understand what people hanging around and talking after church had to do with the preaching. But, then I realised what he was getting at: When we preach a word, we don't just give people an intellectual message - we release God's life and love into their hearts. So, what he was really saying was that the message had deposited life and love into the people's hearts and the fruit was now being shared amongst them in their conversations.

I also believe when we share a word inspired by the Holy Spirit with people, including but not necessarily a bible verse, we are depositing God's love into them as they receive it in faith. When I was a teacher at Bethlehem College in NZ I had a great passion for my job and put my heart and soul into the students. I also was very driven and did not want to fail or fall short in any area. That is why it was such a humbling experience when my Year Eight Science experiments went so horribly wrong in my Friday afternoon class. I was not a Science teacher, nor had I received any training in Science; but nevertheless it was one of my subjects. I hated the fact I had so little knowledge in Science, so despite my best efforts, I would struggle to be able to explain what was happening many times. I walked out of those classes more than a little stressed but also ashamed that, "I had failed", or at least I thought I had.

During this time I would meet with all the new teachers and a lecturer from the teachers college, Ray Stripling, every few weeks. We would eat chocolate cake that his wife had made and discuss how teaching was going. Technically, I wasn't a new teacher because I had taught in both Australia and the UK, but because I was new to the NZ system and hadn't taught for several years, I was also part of the group. As Ray went around the group asking how we were going, he finally got to me. Ray was a very gentle man but also was very prophetic and could *see* what the Lord was showing him and powerfully speak it out. Ray looked at me with deep kindness and love and said, "James, it's not all about performance you know". Ray did not know me that well, and would not have known that I was so driven in my teaching but God had shown him something that day and he felt the need to speak out that one sentence to me. I was caught totally off guard, embarrassingly in front of all the other new teachers, tears began to flow uncontrollably from my eyes. God's word had penetrated my heart and through it He was doing a deep work; replacing the shame and condemnation I was feeling with His comfort and love. God had not just stimulated my intellect, in fact He had side stepped it totally. He had gone straight to my heart and was pouring His love into my brokenness. That is His ministry to our hearts.

Touch can also be an avenue for God's love to be shared from one heart to another. I will always remember when I was at Faith Bible College for a year and was going through a very difficult time. During a service, Sammy the worship leader looked down at me and said, "James, you may not have heard this for a long time; but, I want to tell you that I love you". He then embraced me with a big hug. The words got through; but it was the act of a hug that caused me to burst like a dam and a flood of tears began pouring from me. God was using this man's hug to pour a deposit of love from His heart to mine. The Fathers arms became his as he hugged me and a release of comfort went from him to me. All the pain I had been going through was being washed away.

Another time, when I was at YWAM I was going through a tough time and someone had a word about people needing God's comfort. My heart at this time greatly needed comfort as I was going through a very stressful time. I headed towards the door of the lecture room and nearly made it out before Judy, one of the elders of the base and a precious close friend of Carolyn and I, caught my eye. She looked at me with kindness and asked, "Are you ok?" I turned to her and she gave me a mothers hug, catching me totally off guard and again the tears began to flow as God began to comfort me in my pain. God uses the physical touch of others to deposit His love into our hearts. One of the great difficulties of COVID was people not being able to touch. I am not suggesting that every hug or handshake or pat on the shoulder will bring a deep healing or God's comfort. But touch can be a form of comfort and when it is taken away it takes away an avenue for God to pour His life and love into our hearts.

The love of God is not simply an intellectual idea but it is a substance that goes from the Fathers heart to our hearts. It is a real thing deposited into us as we intertwine with him. *"His love is poured out into our hearts through the Holy Spirit"* (**Romans 5:5**). This love can be deposited into us, through the words or even the touch of someone else.

18. The Heart and True Desire

Psalm 37:4 says that when you *"take delight in the Lord, He will give you the desires of your heart."* I believe as we come into a deeper relationship with the Father, His desires begin to become our desires, and these become an expression of who we truly are.

On the contrary, I have found that religion always tries to make us into something that we are not. We try through effort and will power to become a very spiritual person. We will do things that give us no delight because we believe this is what God expects of us. I am not suggesting that God does not take us through hard times and suffering; He certainly leads us into things that we would never have expected or seen ourselves doing, things too big for us! But, I am referring to doing activities that give us no joy or life because, "it is what God would want". We do it out of a sense of duty. We might believe that to become like Him means to do lots of religious activities, even when they don't seem to be in sync with who we are.

For example, when I first became a Christian I didn't really know who God was, all I knew was that I wanted to

THE HEART AND TRUE DESIRE

do what He wanted me to do. I was a school teacher and I had decided that God would want me to go to a place that I would not enjoy. If I could think up the place and school that I did not want to be at, this was most likely the place where God wanted me to be. That was my line of thinking and how I saw God in those days. At the time, I did not want to go back and live in Sydney where I was brought up; but, I wanted to stay in NZ and get a job in a school that I truly loved. In my mind, I imagined God would do the opposite of what I truly desired. So when all the doors shut on me going back to Sydney and the only door that opened was at a Christian school in Tauranga NZ, I began to see the Fathers true heart for me. That school was where I met my wife and it was also four of the best years of teaching that I ever experienced. It was a place that truly met the desires of my heart.

Often we think, surely the Father of all creation would not be interested in what I am interested in? Surely He does not want us to pursue the things in our hearts? This could not be part of our spiritual act of worship? But that's not my experience.

I have a great love of reptiles, in particular lizards and non venomous snakes. This interest has gripped me since I was a small child running around the unused land in Western Sydney. I loved catching blue tongue lizards, bearded dragons, the occasional water dragon or gecko. As I became a teenager this interest continued only sporadically, mainly because where we lived the land for these lizards was simply no longer there and also I didn't have too many mates who shared my interest. I then became a Christian at 27 and at 30 years old I felt the call to go to Bible College in NZ. Then I was called into a teaching position in a Christian School there. My love for wildlife was still there, but there was only one problem: the forests of NZ were filled with interesting birds with only a few kinds of reptiles, found only in very remote or isolated areas. So this desire was buried away as I pursued more important and spiritual things. Every year when I would return to Australia for holidays, I would experience this little tug at my arm to maybe go on a little herping trip (herping is the act of searching for reptiles). I would head back to my old hunting grounds, not literally, which were now being developed into housing estates and a highway, to see and catch the occasional lizard which were now becoming more rare. It was like God was saying come and do the thing that I put in your heart because it gives me pleasure too.

After living for 15 years in NZ and expecting that I would probably retire in NZ, we got the call to come back to Australia and live in Queensland four years ago. Now, I was super excited about this. Excited for my kids and wife who would experience the land where I had spent my formative years. Also, that we would be closer to my family and that we would experience hot summers, cricket, rugby league, beautiful beaches and of course... reptiles. I taught

THE HEART AND TRUE DESIRE

my kids through my photo albums and stories about the lizards I had caught; so they were aware of this interest. When we came to Queensland we were placed in a spot where wild reptiles were commonly seen again. My kids and I have since been able to experience many kinds of snakes, lizards and other animals like: echidnas, koalas, platypus, wallabies, kangaroos and possums in the wild. Sometimes we will be out in the bush and we will encounter a reptile or other species; and I am reminded of the desire and love that I had for this as a child. I have also since completed a snake catching course and have taken my son on a tour with the local snake catcher, in which we handled and released a number of carpet pythons. When we are driving I am always keeping my eyes out for reptiles and other wildlife. Because of this, we have moved turtles, snakes and lizards off the road on many occasions. Through these experiences I have been reminded how my Father really knows my heart and its desires so well. And the way this has happened has been far more satisfying than I could have ever imagined or invented myself. This is the God of **Ephesians 3:20** who says that, *"He is able to do immeasurably more than all we ask or imagine......"*. Now I know, I know: Paul's talking about spiritual things right - healings, salvations, revivals. But maybe it's also about the little things buried in our hearts that we imagined as a little child that we might experience in this life. Can you relate to this? Maybe it's the Father reminding us of who we are? Of who we were before society or even religion told us how we should look, act and perform. Often the deep things of our beings need to be dug up again as we let Him reveal who we truly are.

Herping for reptiles may be a tiny thing in the context of everything that my life contains but that's the point I'm making. When we know that the Father is interested in those tiny details of our life and meeting those child-like desires tucked away in our hearts, we begin to understand who He is and that the desires of our hearts are important to Him. This is what I have found in my journey as a Spiritual son: *"God loves to fulfil desires that are important and valuable to me; but also, seemingly unimportant or even unspiritual to others"*. Why? Well isn't that what you truly love to awaken in your own children? To see them find out who they truly are? What truly awakens their hearts and makes them unique?

Unspiritual? I don't think so. What's deeply important to you is important to the Father when we are in relationship with Him.

Sometimes we might try to fulfil our own desires, I did this for a great deal of time in my life. We then come to realise that it just doesn't seem to be working. It may even become a very selfish pursuit as we become single minded about this. Since walking with God I have seen so many desires met in me and in such an incredible way. My own way of satisfying my desire was very self focused and I was the centre of attention. When God satisfies the desire of my heart in His way, guess what? He gets the glory and this very event becomes a marker of His goodness and love that we are extremely grateful for and it becomes part of our testimony.

When I was in my late teens and could finally drive, my friends and I got into surfing. We would wake at the crack of dawn, taking the one hour drive every Saturday morning to try and find some waves on the Northern Beaches of Sydney. These were some of the best days of my life, even if we weren't going to win any surfing competitions. I then spent three years working and travelling overseas; but, wherever I went I took my surfboard. I had the surfing bug.

Then in my late twenties, I became a Christian and the priorities of my life began to change. I was still single and enjoying my surfing; so, I decided that I really wanted to join a Christian surfers group. To meet up with a bunch of like minded guys each week whose purpose in life went deeper than just surfing. Despite making some enquiries into this, I just could not get a peace about joining the group nor about moving closer to the beach. It was as if God was saying, "not yet". So I waited, only wanting to move with God as I was learning that is where the peace is. Fast forward a few years, I got the call from God to go to Bible College in Tauranga, NZ. I turned up a week early with my surfboard under my arm as where I was going was near some quality surf beaches. The day I arrived I checked into the hostel where I would spend the week, ran towards the beach and was greeted with some beautiful surfing waves. I spent my first week in NZ catching some incredible waves before I started at Bible College. I didn't know it at the time, but I later learnt that Shark Alley, the beach where the waves had been pumping on that first day- never got swell, it was sheltered on both sides. Likewise, Mount Maunganui, the main beach there, only got occasional swell during the summer yet we had a week of incredible swell. This was a set up from my Father in heaven. I then spent the most amazing year at Faith Bible College in which God did a great work in my life.

After I left Bible College I had almost forgotten about my desire to join a Christian surfers group. But God had not. After I got a job at the local Christian school I met a guy, Anthony, who was a surfer and a teacher at the school. When he found out that I surfed he asked me if I would consider running the Christian surfer group that he had started in the school as he would be going to Israel that year when the big Easter conference was on. I could hardly believe what I was hearing. For several years I had tried unsuccessfully to be part of something like this and now I was being asked to run it. That year I went on some amazing surfing trips with a bunch of young guys and got to share God with them. We got to surf some intense and amazing waves around the North Island of NZ, because the group I had with me were pretty much all good surfers, most of them were better than I was. I ended up doing this for two years and without a doubt a desire in my heart was met. God knew me and had things planned out for me in a way that I would have never imagined or could have fulfilled. Only God can do that!

Since being a Christian I have shared God's word many times and in many places, including in India, NZ and Australia. As well as at churches and at schools, I have shared in a drug and alcohol rehabilitation centre, at the Bible College where I previously attended, at different YWAM bases in NZ, out on the street, in an orphanage, from the roof top of a car in India, in men's groups, at graduation ceremonies and even at friends' weddings. I have even led my own 4 week ministry school called "The School of Sonship" at YWAM Oxford, NZ. I am now writing my second book. Why do I say these things? Hopefully not to boast about anything that I have done. But, these things are a fulfilment of desires that I had as a kid but for years got buried and stolen from my life. The enemy's desire is that if he can't take your soul, he may as well take your God given desires and purpose on this earth.

I loved writing stories as a kid and also acting. I remember having the lead part in the school play, "The Man from Ironbark". I was also made captain of several of the sporting teams that I was in. Then in my teenage years I lost all my confidence and could no longer speak even in front of a small group of people. I disliked myself immensely and did not see any good in me. I had crazy teeth, a big gap between my middle teeth and then big gaps between the next set of teeth that had turned around to look like fangs. I had braces on my teeth and for three years tried to never open my mouth to smile or laugh. Even after I got my braces off my confidence was low. My identity was not in Christ and I was having big struggles with my Dad. I wouldn't have dreamt of sharing or being confident in front of a group *ever again*. I only decided to study Human Movement at University because I was interested in Sport. I had no real intention to be a teacher. Only when I discovered there was nothing that seemed to be of interest or suitable for me in that field, did I decide to do the extra year of study in Health and PE teaching.

It was during this time that I began to get my confidence back in front of groups and started to realise that maybe I could be a school teacher. But to be honest it wasn't for another four years or so when I surrendered my life to Christ that the gift of speaking and leading began to be really given back to me. Just 18 months after becoming a Christian I went to Bible College in NZ, as I have already said, and it was during this time that I found that messages to preach would be downloaded to me. I never had to work hard through intellectual study to get words to preach; they would come from God like a download to my heart. Sometimes in part and sometimes as a whole. All those years ago when I had desires of leading and sharing with people up the front were being and have been restored. I have written plays at school and performed them, preached many messages, coached and refereed many

THE HEART AND TRUE DESIRE

sporting teams, taught kids from 8 years old to 18 years old and written creative stories for my classes. All these things come from a gift that God gave to me. There is nothing I can boast about. But, for years this gift was crushed and just about destroyed. It was God who gave me back this gift and ultimately the desires of my heart.

Of course, when we get a genuine love for God we can get to a point in saying that even if He never meets our desires, we will still follow and love Him. This is a very deep and sacrificial place in our hearts; and I believe God loves to see us come to this point of surrender. Many of us have given up our dream geographical location, occupation, partner or hobby in order to walk in step with the Lord. Others have given up their very lives. This surrender is a noble and necessary thing to do; but, many of us have found that He later rewards this faith by giving us the very desire we surrendered. And if he doesn't we know there is great reward in heaven awaiting us.

When we are truly in Christ, we can know that He has our desires in His hands. He can take these away for a season; but, He can also give them back to us in amazing ways. We may go off in our own ways; but, we learn that true satisfaction in life only comes from letting the Father give us the desires of our hearts and continuing to walk with Him, even when this doesn't feel like it's happening.

Footnote

In the book I make reference to the "Tree of Life" and the "Tree of the Knowledge of Good and Evil" as a way of relating to God. Whilst these were actual trees in the Garden of Eden, I use them as a metaphor to show how sin and the curse has affected the way we *see* and to respond to God and all of life. Eating from the "Tree of the Knowledge of Good and Evil" has entirely changed the way we interact with God and see the world around us. After eating from this tree we became able to judge *good* and *evil* for ourselves without any reference to God. It opened up our ability to have an opinion about everything without having God's heart on the matter at all. Even as Christians this tree is often what we automatically revert to.

I believe part of the good news of Jesus reconciling us back to the Father is that we are being called to live from the "Tree of Life" again, in the way in which Adam and Eve did. In a relationship of complete love and acceptance, where we are led by faith. We can go back to listening in our hearts to what the Holy Spirit is saying to us and no longer just respond from what we hear and see. I have written a chapter on this in more detail in my book *"The Adventure of Faith - A Journey into the Heart of God"*. (2023).

This teaching comes out of revelation that James and Denise Jordan and other teachers in FatherHeart Ministries in NZ have taught on and I acknowledge them as my source for the basis of this teaching. Greater teaching can be found in their resources on the FatherHeart website - *fatherheart.net*.

I also intend to write further on this subject in future books. May the Father reveal the mystery of the Gospel more and more to you as you live and walk in Jesus, the first born son.

Final Thoughts

Our hearts are the very epicentre of who we are. We have been taught that they are unreliable or perhaps only about emotions. Scripture is clear that our hearts are wells that God pours His life into. Our hearts are *us,* when you get behind it all. To ignore our hearts means to live only from our logical minds. To live only from the logical mind is to move away from our very hearts desire and motivation. The Israelites knew the importance of the heart and its centrality to who we really are. They did not see it as dangerous or simply evil and deceptive. Yes, evil comes from the heart. Yes, our hearts can be deceptive. But, that is because our hearts were orphaned from God the Father and they lost their true purpose. When our hearts are submitted to Father God and under the lead of the Holy Spirit they are rich storehouses for His love, joy and compassion.

Our hearts are the filter for everything we pour into them. They are like wells of salt and fresh water where both are mixed together. If we dismiss our hearts entirely, you miss out on the lovely fresh water - just so you can get rid of the salt water. The church has often called out the salt water and in doing so dismissed the beautiful fresh water that lies within our hearts; The Fathers: love, desire and motives. When we don't recognise the goodness of our hearts we can not have the Fathers heart for the world.

May we see our hearts as God intended and may we be circumcised in our hearts as the apostle Paul encouraged us to be. That our walk with God may be one that is heart to heart, and not simply one of knowledge and trying to get our theology *'right'*.

God bless,
– *James*

Appendices

Appendix 1 - Example of a Heart Forgiveness Letter

Dear Mum,

It has only been a few months since you were laid to rest after your 7 week battle with pancreatic cancer. I was glad I could be with you over that time and get to say some of the things I needed to say, but it is still raw.

I want to ask your forgiveness for some of the things I couldn't really say to you for fear of causing hurt and unnecessary anguish.

I know you and Dad did your best to raise me & my 2 brothers by providing opportunities to flourish. However yours was a generation where true feelings were not always acknowledged, but only on how you performed.

You made me beautiful clothes and knitted colourful jerseys & cardigans.

As a preschooler you took photos of me in beautiful dresses, but didn't always tell me I was loved. I look at photos now and wonder if it was just for show.

You came to my swimming sports and netball games when I was in my teens. I never heard you congratulating me, but I did hear you boasting to my Aunt that I had done well in my championships. Maybe you thought I would get a big head if you told me you were proud of me.

I needed you to ask me about my dreams and listen to my real fears and not be dismissive. I heard years later how hard it was for you to say goodbye to me when leaving me in Christchurch for my University studies, after travelling from another city 6 hours away. In fact you said to a neighbour you cried on your way home but I never knew that separation was hard for you as it was for me. I had to be brave and make my own way in a new city. I was only 17.

I used to write letters home telling you of my achievements as I felt I needed your approval to be accepted.

As I've matured and discovered the love of my Heavenly Father, I know I'm totally accepted for who I am and not for what I have to strive for. I realise it was part of the generation you were brought up in not having any encouragement from your parents for fear of pride.

I forgive you for not listening to my fears and ambitions and therefore not giving me all I needed from you as a Mum. You were caring and you sacrificed much for me to have dancing and piano lessons that you never had. Maybe you lived your life through me?

— *Your loving daughter*

Sources Referenced

Jordan, J (2012). *Sonship - A Journey into the Father's Heart*. Taupo, NZ: Tree of Life Media

Arnold, J. (1995). *The Father's Blessing*. Orlando: Creation House.

Collins, (1995). *Creation/Evolution, Issue 36,* Summer, 1995, p. 15-23.

www.ingramcontent.com/pod-product-compliance
Lightning Source LLC
Chambersburg PA
CBHW062051290426
44109CB00027B/2789